Good Judgment

**The new judge's guide to dog showing
and the showring**

Peggy Grayson

*The pleasure of looking at a beautiful animal is great, but the
pleasure of looking at two beautiful animals is greater, and the
pleasure of comparing them is greatest.*

William McCandlish

Good Judgment

The new judge's guide to dog showing and the showring

Peggy Grayson

KINGDOM

Contents

The book has been colour coded to help you find relevant sections of illustrations. The colours below correspond to coloured tabs at the top left and right of each page. To find the section you want, simply look for the matching coloured tab.

Author's Note

This book has been written not only at the request of people starting on their judging careers, but also at the suggestion of friends who steward regularly and find how unprepared many new judges are for their task. It is based on over 50 years of judging experience and, although the thoughts expressed and the information given may be somewhat personal, they will be found to be sound and workable.

This is a book of the basics which everyone should know before setting out to judge.

When this book was written, the columns of the dog press were full of complaints about bad judging, ignorant judging and the like, and much criticism of the type and soundness of the dogs being placed.

I hope that this book will help the judges of the future to understand the great responsibility that rests on their shoulders as they step into the ring and, hopefully, assist in making a sound and knowledgeable panel for the continuance of dog shows into the next century.

Throughout the book, the word 'he' has been used when referring to the judge, steward or dog owner. This is for ease of reading only, and is not intended in any way to undervalue the skill and ability of the many excellent ladies who contribute so much to dog showing and judging.

Peggy Grayson

Acknowledgements

The author would like to thank the following for their help with the loan of dogs or photographs:

Mr and Mrs L. Byles
Mr G. Corish and Mr M. Hoad
David Dalton
Mrs Dixon
Thomas Fall
Mrs Mary le Gallais
Mr and Mrs Peter Harper
Mrs Sheila Jakeman
Mrs Jennings
Carol Ann Johnson
Mr D. Kitchener
Miss Jackie Kitchener
Mr and Mrs D. Osborne and Mrs Ina Morton
Diane Pearce

Special thanks to Angela Begg, who drew the illustrations, and Robert Smith, who took most of the the photographs

The quotations at the head of the chapters are taken from *Dog Show Maxims*, written in the 1920s by William McCandlish, one of the great all-rounders of his day, and published by Popular Dogs Publishing Co. Limited.

Preface

Dog shows in truth, would have no continuance and no life in them if it were not for judges. Judging is at the heart of dog shows and pumps the blood that makes the life of the whole system.

William McCandlish

When dog shows started in 1859, the pressing need was for people to judge at them. The first show, held in Newcastle, solved the problem neatly by having the organisers judge the show and win the major prizes! This sort of thing could not go on forever and, as the numbers of shows increased, more and more people were required to enter the ranks of judges.

Dog shows were conceived some years after agricultural events had been organised for other livestock, and the organisers had to rely on those gentlemen who had bred and worked sporting dogs, many of whom were already established judges of horses, cattle, sheep, pigs, poultry, small stock and/or pigeons. Later they were joined in the judging ranks by men who had worked their way up from kennel boy through to kennel manager, or from being the odd job boy on shoots to the head gamekeeper. As the years went on it became acceptable for ladies, too, to be invited to judge.

The foundation of The Kennel Club in 1873 resulted in this body then overseeing the matter of judges. Over the past century and a quarter it has taken more and more part in who should, and who should not, be accepted to judge at championship level.

However, The Kennel Club makes no rules as to who judges shows beneath championship status, and this is where the aspiring novice judges begin to get their experience.

With so little chance for the new judge to gain experience and find out what is required, and how to set about things, it seemed that a book was needed which could assist the newcomer to start on the right lines and judge wisely and well. Here it is!

The author with the Best of Breed Irish Red and White Setter, Sh. Ch. Spyrefire
Pandora's Box, at the Gundog Breeds of Scotland Championship Show 1995.
Photograph by Carol Prangle

Chapter One

The Making of a Judge

The first requirement of the great bulk of exhibitors is that there shall be honest judging, and the second requirement is that the judging shall be competent.

William McCandlish

In the past, judges were drawn from two sources, people who were successful breeders and exhibitors in their own right, and those who had 'got their hands dirty'. The former were owners of kennels of some years' standing, who were seen to produce high class stock that had proved itself in the ring, and so were invited to officiate in their breed. Many were diffident about accepting and some well-known people never judged at all, preferring only to breed and exhibit at the highest level. The latter started as the most lowly kennelmaid or boy and progressed up the ladder to become head kennelmaid or man, or kennel manager. They served a long apprenticeship under the authoritarian but knowledgeable rule of the owner and his head man or woman. Such people either stayed as employees at famous kennels, or branched out on their own as breeders and exhibitors, many with sidelines such as boarding or trimming to finance their entry fees and show expenses.

By their constant and close association with dogs, handling dozens of different dogs and puppies in every kind of situation and in sickness and in health, they really understood their craft and could take their place with honour beside those whose kennels were household names. Secretaries and officials of canine societies kept their eyes open for potential judges, and it was not long before these people were invited to judge a club match. The matches were usually held in the back room of a pub, where the onlookers would be deep in dog knowledge and not slow to tell fledgling judges where they had gone wrong, and not slow either to praise a good decision.

The word would be passed round that 'young so-and-so' showed a bit of an aptitude for judging. Invitations to judge other clubs' matches would follow, and from this an invitation to judge a sanction show. The progress was slow and a number of such engagements would have to be undertaken before the hopeful judge was offered classes in his own breed or breeds, or the ones with which he had been most associated.

A well-turned out Bichon Frisé, owner and judge!

Sanction and limited shows were a grand apprenticeship. Newcomers got to put their hands on the good, bad and indifferent dogs of many breeds. The ringside being deep in dog knowledge, the new judge had to think carefully through his deliberations before reaching a decision. Making mistakes, and having them corrected by the more knowledgeable, was an invaluable way to gain experience and stopped the newer judge from getting big headed!

Today, everything is very different. There is no hierarchy in the world of dogs, as the large kennels and the people with money and interest to sustain good breeding programmes have almost vanished. Gone, too, are most of the knowledgeable older men and women, and with them most of the sanction and limited shows. Many modern exhibitors are interested only in qualifying for Crufts, and so shun shows that they feel do not count.

You, today's aspiring judge, probably have been associated with one breed and, hopefully, you have collected, read and assimilated all the books and other material on that breed. For the potential judge there is no substitute for a good 'doggy' library. Borrow or buy all the books you can and read them. Buy a set of standards from The Kennel Club and, taking one group at a time, study the descriptions in depth. You may not wish to judge anything but your own breed, but this cannot be done satisfactorily unless you know about other breeds; a good all-round knowledge of the subject is essential. Some useful videos are also available about various breeds. You should buy also a good veterinary book containing illustrations of skeletons, muscle formation, and the whereabouts of all the parts, both inside and outside the dog, together with a glossary of terms.

Most aspiring judges start by judging their own breed, so visit as many kennels and see as many dogs and puppies of your chosen breed as possible. A good way to learn about dogs and judging dogs is to sit at the ringside and watch. A solitary stint observing movement, size, balance, preparation, handling and the way various judges go about their task is an essential part of a would-be judge's education. It is useless to sit with a companion, as you are bound to chat and your eyes will stray from the ring. After exhibiting, do not pack up and go home as soon as your class is finished. Make your dog comfortable, and then spend an hour or so at the ringside.

Stewarding is said to be a good preparation for judging, but in breeds of small numbers the stewards are so busy attending to their own duties that there is little time left to study the breed in the ring or the way the judge of the day performs. In breeds of large numbers, however, usually there is plenty of time to watch the proceedings and, as you are in the ring, you have the advantage of closer contact with the dogs than people at the ringside. Stewarding also teaches you how to manage a ring and, by observing the judges for whom you work, to learn at first hand some of the problems you will encounter when you take the centre of the ring in your turn.

The age of the seminar is now with us, and many meetings are well organised and have good speakers and tutors to help educate aspiring judges. For your first visits to such events, choose the breed or breeds in which you are interested or with which you have had some contact, and leave the more exotic or obscure breeds until you have more basic knowledge.

Before you go into the ring, it is essential to have studied the basics well: to know the construction of the dog, how to go over a dog, to know what you are looking for when you put your hands on the dog, to appreciate the difference between good and bad movement, to spot quality and to understand type. You must be able to keep your nerve, maintaining an unswerving purpose to put up those dogs which you consider to be the best on the day and not to be sidetracked.

Examine your motives for wanting to judge. Do you have a fund of knowledge that you can put to good use? Can you serve your chosen breed by taking on judging engagements for it? Will you be able to make decisions that will be seen as fair, unbiased and showing a good grounding in the breed? Can you recognise faults or failings and put them in perspective in your mind, before making your placings? Unless you feel you can contribute something to your breed as a judge, perhaps you are not yet ready for the task.

A good motto for the aspiring judge is, 'Ask not what dogs can do for you but what you can do for dogs.' Judging should not be an ego trip but a serious job of work in the interest of the pedigree dog. Nothing is more unnerving than to take on a task and then find one is not well enough prepared to carry it through. Those who want to judge because it makes them feel important to stand in the middle of the ring, irrespective of whether they have enough knowledge to take on an assignment, are unlikely to make a success of the job.

The temptation in this age of speed is to seek to judge before you are really ready to undertake the task. A judge's job is an onerous one. People will have paid good money for your opinion, but will they value it if you take on the job too soon without the necessary experience? Judges are not there to choose which dog appeals to

What to look for and how to find it

1. **Look at the dog in profile to determine proportion, conformation and balance.**

2. **Look at the dog from the front to see width and development of chest, shoulder placement and straightness of legs.**

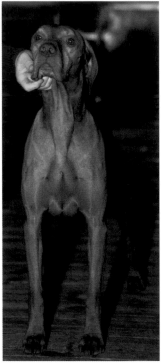

3. **Look at the dog from the rear to see width and strength of quarters and hock placement.**

4. Go to the dog's head. Speak to the dog, take its head in your hands and lift lips to check dentition (ask the handler of breeds such as German Shepherd to do this). Ask a Chow Chow's handler to open its mouth so that you can see its colour.

5. Take the dog's head in your hands to check eye shape, colour, placement and expression. Check ear shape and shape of skull.

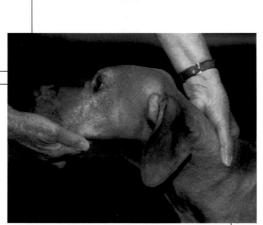

6. Look at the head in profile to check ratio of skull to foreface in relation to the breed you are judging. Check throat to see it is clean in breeds where this is demanded, or has the characteristic fold or dewlap required by other breeds.

What to look for and how to find it

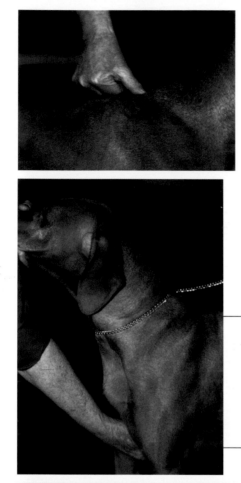

7. **Feel the meeting point of the shoulder blades (scapula). This junction is termed 'the withers'. The lay of the shoulder can be determined by placement of withers.**
   (See pages 76 and 77 on the use of the plumbline.)

8. **Check for correct formation of chest and brisket and that there is sufficient heart room.**

9. **Check spring of rib.**

10. Feel for well-developed back muscles, necessary to hold topline in place.

11. Check for shape of feet, depth of pads and evenness of wear.

12. Check for width, depth and strength of loin.

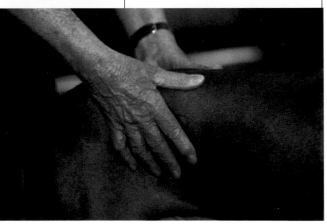

What to look for and how to find it

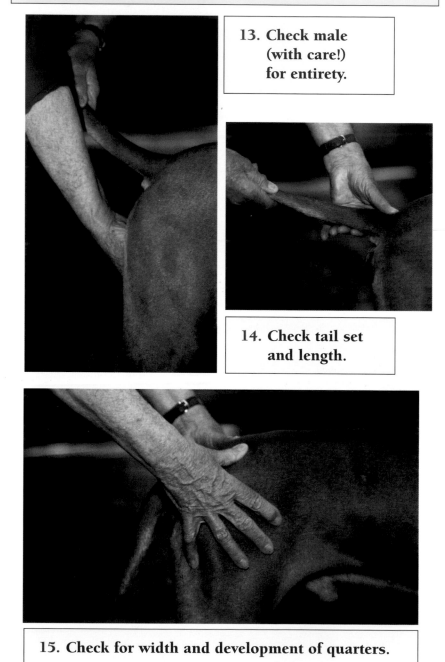

13. Check male (with care!) for entirety.

14. Check tail set and length.

15. Check for width and development of quarters.

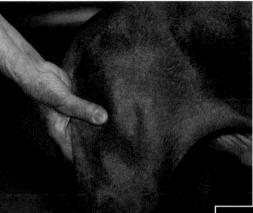

16. Check for development of muscle in the thighs.

17. Check for correct construction and muscling of second thigh.

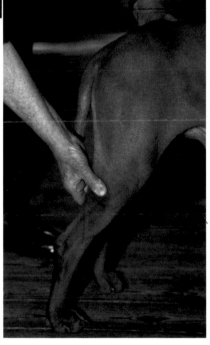

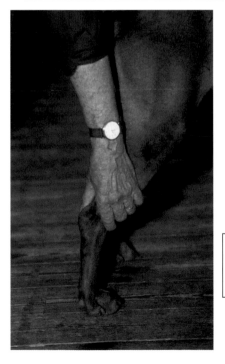

18. Check to feel hock joint is strong.

The dog used as a model is Hungarian Viszla Sh. Ch. Pitzwarren Levi, belonging to Mr and Mrs Harper.

them, nor to indulge in their own little fads and fancies, such as 'Anything I put up must have a lovely head', or 'I would never place a dog that was out of coat', or 'My breed is of a certain colouration, I would never put up a dog with less than perfect markings', and so on. The dog must be judged as a whole against the Breed Standard and on its appearance and performance on the day.

Do not be afraid to refuse the first offer to judge if you have any reservations about whether you are ready to take on the task. Do not think that by refusing you will never be asked again. Not so: giving the reason for refusal, that you do not feel quite ready, will win you praise, and the word will spread that you have a responsible attitude to the task. Another invitation will arrive later and this you may feel you can accept.

What makes you so sure you will make a good judge? Have you an 'eye' for a dog? Yes, there really is such a thing. Just as some people have a gift for breeding, always seeming to know which combination of the bloodlines will produce winners, and achieving just that year after year, so some people are born with an eye for balance, proportion and conformation, and instinctively know quality when they see it. Such people see these things not only in dogs but in other animals, gardens, architecture, fashions, paintings or house fittings. They are appreciative of that which fits comfortably into the mind's eye, and eschew the grotesque, gaudy, unbalanced, unfinished or mediocre. Lucky indeed are those born with this critical faculty, the ability to spot the best, and they must nourish it and use it for the betterment of pedigree dogs.

Can people be taught to judge? This is an oft-debated point. For those who have a natural 'eye' there is little problem, for they assimilate breed points easily and their 'eye' has already given them a head start in recognising good conformation and soundness. For the dedicated dog person who does not have a natural 'eye', a little more preparation is necessary. However, with a willingness to learn and serve a good apprenticeship, such enthusiasts can in time become very efficient and successful in judging their chosen breeds.

In the United Kingdom at the time of writing, there is no official training scheme for judges. Many other countries have schemes but the success of these depends largely on the type and quality of the scheme and who trains the potential judges. Whilst I have seen and admired many overseas judges of high standing doing excellent jobs in the centre of the ring, I feel that such people are those with a natural 'eye' who would have made top class judges anyway. Some others, who have the same training and passed the same scrutiny, fall very far short of doing a competent job.

Rottweiler Ch. Fernwood Fallon, owned by Miss D Rowell

Seminars for judges in this country have only been organised in any number since the late 1980s, and these do go some way to educating would-be judges to understand their task. Such gatherings are only of use, however, if the content is carefully chosen and the tutors soundly versed in their breed and capable of communicating their knowledge in an effective manner.

Honesty and integrity in judging are paramount. As a new judge, you need to start your career firm of purpose. There are, of course, as in all careers or walks of life, easy ways to success. Inducements may be offered to join this or that faction within a breed (most breeds, sadly, have people pulling in different directions). You might receive suggestions about which clubs to join; how to get on a particular committee; the functions to attend where, you will be told, 'the goodies are handed out'. You will be advised to frequent the bar at shows, never to disagree with the mighty, always be seen at the right place at the right time, be ready to please. Favours may be offered for favours. You will be told that it is acceptable to ask for judging engagements, on the grounds that 'you won't get if you don't ask'. To go down any of these roads is to start on a very slippery slope indeed.

Happily, this Primrose Path is taken only by those few whose ambition is so overweening, or whose confidence in their own ability so poor, that they feel they will never get the volume of engagements they crave unless they make all the moves.

Judges are not there to give favours, pay off old scores, pick out friends or leave out enemies. They must not 'run scared' and choose the first dog that presents a reasonable appearance because the handler is glaring at them in a belligerent manner, nor search along the line to try to recognise a well-known winner or familiar face at the end of the lead. There is no easy path to good judging. Well done, it is a hard job of work, demanding not only well-founded knowledge but stamina and intense concentration. If people who want to judge cannot recognise that, they should find another occupation.

The collecting of judging appointments can become an all-absorbing passion. It can be a drug as addictive as tobacco, alcohol or gambling – just as heady and difficult to combat as any other addiction. Over a lifetime in dogs, I have seen marriages break up because of the obsession of one party to get more and more engagements. I have seen marriages or partnerships made because to attach oneself to a person who is successful and influential in the world of dogs can accelerate the process up the judging ladder. Sadly, I have also known many people so incapable of saying 'no' to any and every invitation that they have ruined their health.

Judging, like any other interesting, pleasurable and worthwhile occupation, must be kept in perspective. Those who pursue a career as a judge need to be able to sleep peacefully at night in the sure and certain knowledge that they have done the job fairly and to the best of their ability.

Remember, as well as being show dogs, the animals you see will all be well-loved pets, such as Cavalier King Charles Spaniel Muffity Morgana, owned by Mrs Hall.

Chapter Two

The First Invitation

The nervousness of starting is recovered only if a sound and simple formula is adopted.

William McCandlish

Although you will receive your first invitation to judge with excitement and, perhaps, a little apprehension, you need to approach the situation in a businesslike manner. There are certain Kennel Club rules to be observed about the receiving and accepting of judging engagements and these are as follows.

The judge must receive from the secretary a letter of invitation stating the date, time and place of the show, and the number of classes of the breed to be judged. The invited judge must write back accepting the invitation and will later receive, probably after the club's next committee meeting, another letter stating that he has been accepted to judge. Until those three letters have been sent and received, there is no judging contract.

However, once the three letters have passed between the parties, the judge may not back out except for a very good reason such as health, family problems, or something quite outside his control. If he does not turn up to judge on the day, he can be fined by The Kennel Club for breaking the contract and may also be dropped from his breed club's judging list.

That is the official line, but there are other considerations. Secretaries have to keep their paperwork up-to-date, so it is polite and helpful to reply to invitations within 48 hours of receiving them, especially if you cannot accept, as the secretary then has the job of finding another name.

The invitation may state that the society expects the invited judge not to judge the breed at another show within six, or sometimes twelve, months before the date of their show, or maybe not to judge at shows within 50 or even 100 miles' radius of the venue. Now do check the venue, as so many societies hold their show many miles from the named base.

Not all societies ask this but it is wise, if you are a newcomer just starting out, not to accept two engagements in the same area, as you should always think of the effect on entries. Two engagements close together will undoubtedly mean that one show or the other will have a small entry. However keen you are to judge, do pace yourself and space the engagements out across the country.

This is Staffordshire Bull Terrier Ch. Boldmore Finbar Fury, owned by Mr Clarke.

Back to that first invitation. The letter will read something like this:

I am instructed by the committee of the Muddlecombe Canine Society to invite you to judge three classes of Mousehounds on Sunday July 31st 1998 at the Drill Hall, Muddlecombe, judging to commence at 10am. I hope you will be able to accept.

You must reply in a similar tone, thus:

Please thank the committee of the Muddlecombe Canine Society for their kind invitation to judge three classes of Mousehounds at their show to be held at the Drill Hall, Muddlecombe, on Sunday July 31st 1998, judging to start at 10am. I am pleased to be able to accept.

25

If you repeat the wording of the invitation, there can be no misunderstandings. I do urge you to take a copy of your answer and clip it to the invitation.

Nearer the time, the secretary should send you a schedule with the number of dogs entered in each class you are to judge, a car pass if necessary, a complimentary pass and sometimes the lunch ticket, although this is usually collected at the show. If you want to take a companion, do tell the secretary in your letter of acceptance. Most canine societies are very hospitable and usually give you two lunch tickets as long as they are aware you will be accompanied.

The day of the show

Get an early night, and do watch your diet. Heavy meals on a nervous stomach can cause much discomfort, so have a light supper and then in the morning a light but sustaining breakfast. You would be wise to abstain from any large intake of alcohol the previous evening. A peaceful night's sleep will make you feel ready for the task ahead.

Work out your mode of transport well in advance. If driving yourself, map out the route and estimate how long the journey will take, then add half an hour for delays. Plan to get to the show at least half an hour before you are due to start judging as this gives you time to settle down. If a friend is driving, make sure they come in good time. Make sure the vehicle is in good order, has a full petrol tank and that tyres, oil and water are all checked.

If travelling by public transport, make sure the train or bus times are correct and it might be wise to buy your ticket in advance and book a seat. Do not forget the return journey, and choose a later rather than earlier train or bus in case you are held up at the show. Do not expect travel expenses until you are more experienced and can judge several breeds; shows cannot afford to reimburse the new judge who is just learning his trade.

At the show, go to the secretary's table where you will be received by a show official, probably the President, Chairman or show manager. The secretary will be busy, but is sure to stop work to welcome you.

You will be offered coffee or tea and do accept, as a warm drink helps to drown the butterflies that go with the job! In the reception area you will meet the other judges, some of whom may also be new, and a pleasant chat helps to dispel the tension.

Do visit the 'facilities'! You might as well be comfortable before entering the ring, and ladies can see to their hair and make up, and gentlemen tidy themselves.

Back at the secretary's table you will given a judge's badge and judging book and be introduced to your steward who will take you to your ring. If you are following another judge, do not enter the ring until he has finished judging, collected up his papers and left the ring. It is very bad manners to hustle the preceding judge so that you can get on with your classes.

Once in the ring, take a seat at the table and put out your judging book, note book or recorder, pen or pencil, and spectacles should you need these. Put on your judge's badge. Sometimes this is a rosette with long tails. Pin the tails to the back of the badge so they do not flap in the faces of the exhibits. At one time a bowl of water, soap, disinfectant and a towel were supplied to all judges but this is seldom done now and usually there is a carton of wipes on each table. Do not start judging until you have some method of cleaning your hands. By now you may be feeling nervous and

A typical entry in a judging book.

Judging the Bull Breeds

The bull (*brachycephalic*) breeds have many characteristics in common in head properties, width of chest and general make and shape. The French Bulldog illustrates how these breeds should be judged.

1. **The first impression of the head, looking at expression and the ear carriage.**

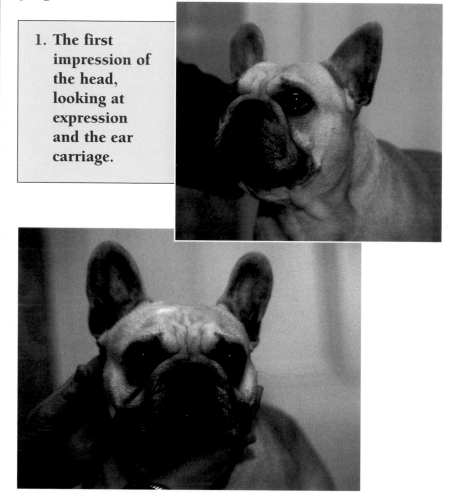

2. **Checking eyes and packing under them, looking for wide open nostrils and well fitted flews (lips), which should not hang too loose or hang below the jaw line.**

3. Feeling depth of stop and flatness of skull between the ears.

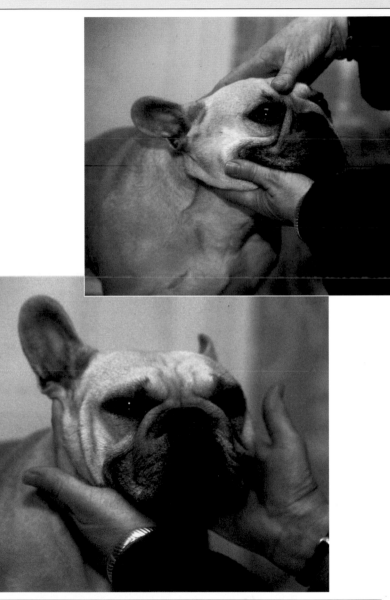

4. Hands feeling width of underjaw and steadying head ready to check jaw and dentition.

Judging the Bull Breeds

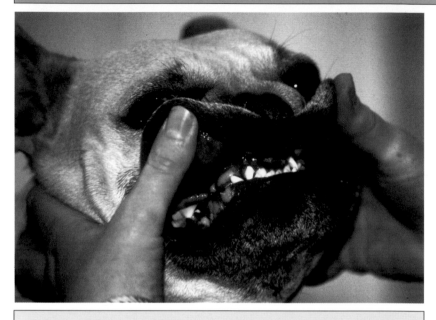

5. The correct method of handling the mouth of the brachycephalic breeds. Place both hands under the lower jaw and use the thumbs to flip up the flews to reveal not only the teeth but the all-important jaw line on either side. It is quite impossible to judge whether the jaw is wry or not merely by looking at or feeling the front teeth.

6. Feeling depth and width of chest, checking legs are straight, and feet the right shape.

7. Feeling the neck and shoulder line, depth of rib and cut up. Next check the hind limbs and bend of the stifle.

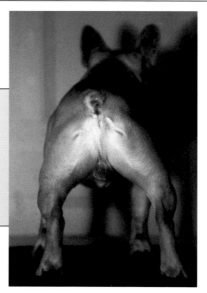

9. Last look at the rear, checking for straight hocks. This chap is standing rather too wide behind.

31

this is only natural: people who say they do not feel nervous when tackling their first few engagements seldom make good judges. Take several very deep breaths, and you will be surprised how you calm down.

The judging book

There are several types of judging book used at open shows but the *Our Dogs* version is the most popular. Do study the book before you start judging and make sure you know whether the winning numbers should run across or down the strips.

All judging books have space for comments and you can use this to make the notes that you will need later to write your critique. However, space in these books is somewhat cramped so it is wise to provide yourself with a reporter's notebook.

Many judges now use a hand-held recorder, and it is up to you if you opt for one of these. I tried this when they first came out, but somehow the whole tape got wiped off after judging ten classes at a championship show – a nightmare! So it was back to the notebook and pencil again. Take both pen and pencil, as the ink might run out in one, or the lead break in the other.

You are in sole charge of your judging book. Stewards should not write in any numbers except those of the absentees, which they may enter if you request them to do so. Do not allow stewards to fill in your slips. This is often seen to be done but is incorrect: the judge's book is just that, your property and your responsibility. You may see the more blasé judges signing all the slips in their judging books while sitting in the reception area. This is technically incorrect, as no slip should be signed until the class is over.

You will find three columns on each page in which to write the numbers of the placed dogs. The first column is the judge's check on the placed dogs, and you must sign the other two slips, one for the ring award board and one for the secretary's office. It is vital that this procedure is carried out, as the catalogues are marked from the slips, and two copies sent to The Kennel Club. It is very important that the information is correct.

Mark up your book as soon as you have lined up your winners. Make sure that at the end of your judging you mark down the numbers of the Best of Breed, Best of Opposite Sex and Best Puppy on all the slips. You must fill in both slips, as well as the space provided for the judge which you will need when you are writing your critique. Tear off the slips on the perforated line nearest to your own line of numbers and give the two slips, still joined together, to the steward.

One or two difficulties may occur. Firstly, there are the exhibitors who arrive late and miss their class and, as it is the only class for which they are entered, they cannot transfer to another class. Sometimes an exhibitor enters in the wrong class. For example, if the dog is over 12 calendar months of age but has been entered in Minor Puppy or Puppy, it may be transferred to the junior class. Other incorrectly-entered dogs may be transferred to the open class.

No exhibitors who have made an entry can be barred from taking part in the class for which they have paid, even if both you and the steward know that they are ineligible. Make a note of this fact and give it to the secretary who will send a report to The Kennel Club; it is up to them to deal with this matter.

Before you leave you will be given a catalogue. This may have been marked up for you by the steward during the judging, or you may receive one from the secretary which may or may not be marked. Take great care of your judging book as you need to consult this for the winning numbers.

After the judging

At the conclusion of your classes, do not linger in the ring as another judge may be waiting to take over. Check that you have collected all your belongings and, if the steward is not taking you to lunch, do remember to thank him for his help. Before leaving, it is appreciated if you go to the secretary's table and thank the officials for inviting you and for a nice day.

Before you start for home, let yourself relax – you will be rather wound-up with all the excitement.

Chapter Three

Managing Your Ring

The principal feature of a dog show is the judging, and, therefore, the arena for judging should be well staged and attractive.

William McCandlish

When sitting at your table waiting to start judging, take a good look at your ring and its particular shape and size. Many open shows these days classify a very large number of breeds, and at indoor shows this can lead to smaller rings than are suitable in an effort to cram all the dogs and judging into the available area.

Oblong rings are the best as you have two long sides down which you can see the dogs move. However, few venues can accommodate rings of this shape and you are more likely to have a square ring. This will be divided from the public or the next ring by ropes or plastic ribbons. If it is separated from the public, then chairs or benches will be provided so that people can sit and watch the proceedings.

Sometimes the back of your ring will be against a wall, and sometimes you will be at the end of a line of rings with two sides bounded by walls.

All these facts must be taken into consideration when judging, as not only must the dogs be judged, but they should be moved and placed so that the ringside can observe what is happening.

The ground will never be as slippery at outdoor shows as indoor venues often prove to be, although there will always be the exhibitor who complains that the ground is uneven, has thistles, the grass is too long or too short and so on. Outdoor rings are far the best in which to assess movement. However, even the best of these can have its drawbacks, especially on a windy day when the breeze plays havoc with the coats of long-haired breeds and judging takes a little longer.

When judging outside in sunny weather, line up the dogs facing the sun so that you have your back to the sun. Never try to judge

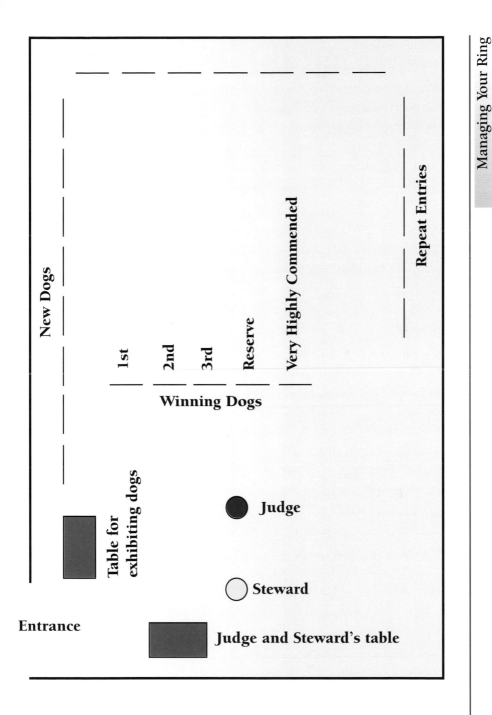

The Showring

with the sun in your eyes. If the judge's table is set facing the sun, ask for it to be moved so that the sun is behind it. All outdoor shows have wet weather accommodation, so check with the steward to find where your wet weather ring is situated, especially if it looks as though rain is on the way.

Indoors, the floor may be like that of the modern sports hall, many of which are used for various ball games and have lines painted in bright colours. These can prove a great hazard as some dogs hate them and resolutely refuse to move. I once judged a class of English Setters, and the dogs literally stood on their claws with horrified expressions, unable to move an inch. I took the whole class outside in the rain to judge the movement although, strictly speaking, one is not supposed to judge the exhibits outside the designated area. However, I felt that it was the only fair way to deal with the situation. In cases like this, it is better to ask for some rubber matting or similar and hope that something is available.

Some of the newer halls are carpeted, but many of the small village halls are used for a number of purposes and are slippery. In this case, the organisers should place strips of rubber matting in strategic positions all around the ring so that exhibits can move round safely, plus a strip down the centre or in a triangular shape. In these smaller rings, you may find it best to ask the exhibitors to move their dogs twice up and down the centre mat while you walk to the side and view the dogs in profile as they make the second trip. Some exhibitors seem to think that the mat is for them to walk on while the dogs slip and slide on the shiny floor.

There may be a separate small table to use when judging the small breeds or 'table dogs' which should be set to the left of your judge's table. Not all shows provide a separate table, and you may have to use one corner of the judge's table. Usually a rubber mat or small square of carpet is provided to give the dog a grip.

Sometimes an exhibitor is competing in another ring although having a dog entered in the class you are about to judge, and you may be asked if you will wait until the exhibitor can appear. There is no obligation for you to do this, but it is courteous to give the exhibitor five minutes' grace. Ask your steward to tell the other entrants that there is a hold up and for what reason. Any longer than five minutes is unfair to the waiting exhibitors and their dogs and, although it may seem hard to go on with a class when one of the participants is actually at the show, it is not your responsibility if classes clash.

The time has come to start your task. All your nervousness will disappear as soon as you get in the ring with the breed with which you are so familiar: your breed, the one you are considered capable of judging.

Lord of all he surveys! Dachshund Ch. Marictur Mr Moto, owned by Mrs S Hunt and bred by Margaret Turner.

Step confidently into the middle of the ring, and be prepared for the steward to announce you as the judge. This is happening more and more, so do not let it upset you, but smile and acknowledge the ripple of applause that follows.

Stand and take a good look at the dogs, then walk down the ring observing line, size, stance and balance before going back to the centre and asking exhibitors to move their dogs around the ring. You

Expression is important

Expression denotes character; without the correct expression for a breed, some of the character is lost. Hence the old saying, 'the dog must look at you right'.

1. **The self-assured and fearless gaze of the Rottweiler.**

2. **The expression of the Basset Hound is calm and serious.**

3. **The alert, fearless and gay expression of the Cairn Terrier.**

4. **The kindly expression of the Golden Retriever.**

Coated breeds

On breeds which have heavy coats or breeds with trimmed coats the judge needs to feel the structure under the coat. Clever grooming can hide faults from a judge who does not take the trouble to go over the dog thoroughly.

1. The Rough Collie.

2. The Old English Sheepdog.

3. The Chow Chow. Mrs Sheila Jakeman's Tanlap True Target.

4. The Bichon Frise. Fougere Baggy Britches owned by Mrs J Stapley.

Pigmentation

Full pigmentation is desirable in all breeds.

1. **The brilliant white of the Maltese coat is set off by the dark brown eyes, with black eye rims and dark halos, jet black nose and black pads to the feet.**

2. **The black spotted Dalmatians seen here have dark eyes with black eye rims and jet black noses. The nails can be black or white. Liver spotted Dalmatians have amber eyes, and liver eye rims and noses. Nails may be liver or white.**

3. Liver coloured dogs always have liver noses and eye rims and eyes to tone with the coat, as shown here by Mrs Ina Morgan's Field Spaniel Sh. Ch. Shirmal Chocolate Soldier. The same is true of liver and tan, liver and white, liver, white and tan or liver roan dogs.

4. Chow Chows have blue/black gums, tongues and roofs to their mouths. It is correct to ask the handler to show the teeth and mouth in this breed.

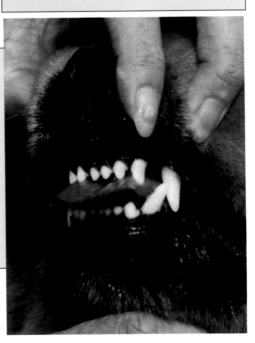

may require them to do this once or twice, but on very hot days do not ask the exhibits to move more than is absolutely necessary. This is particularly important if you are judging one of the brachycephalic breeds, that is, those with short faces such as Bulldogs, French Bulldogs, Pugs and Pekingese which are liable to be badly affected by prolonged exposure to hot sun.

Standing with your back to the judge's table, which is the centre of your world for the time being, you will find that it is easier to have all new dogs standing to your left.

The exhibits come forward one at a time for examination and individual movement and, when that is completed, join on the end of the line. The line then shuffles forward; you see the next dog and the process is repeated until all the dogs have been examined and the first dog is at the head of the line again. Make each exhibitor stand their dog well away from the table so that you can get a good view of the animal. It also allows the ringside to see each dog clearly.

Make sure you know how many cards are to be awarded, decide where you want your final line-up to stand and tell your steward who, when you call your winners out, will place them in the spot you have indicated in the centre of the ring from left to right facing the ringside where the most spectators are congregated.

The steward should hand you your judging book, note book and pen, but if he is working single-handed you may have to fetch these from the judging table. Mark the numbers of the winners clearly in your judging book. While you are thus engaged the steward should be marking his award sheet with the numbers. The prize cards should not be handed out until you have filled in your book and signed the page. They should be given out from left to right by the steward, who should call the winners' numbers in a clear voice so that the ringside can mark their catalogues.

The class is not officially over until you have completed the relevant page in your judge's book and signed it. It is important that these procedures are followed as the last two exhibitors in line have a nasty habit of disappearing before their numbers are taken, particularly if they are annoyed at being placed down the line! If any exhibitor does leave your chosen line-up before you have marked your book, ask the steward to call them back and insist that they stay there until you have taken their numbers.

You will then be free to take notes on your placed dogs for use when writing your critique.

Once the ring is cleared of the first class the entrants for the next class are called in and the whole procedure takes place again. Before you go to the centre, allow the steward to assemble the new class and check the numbers and then come back to indicate to you that all is ready. To rush in and start proceedings before the numbers have all been checked is incorrect.

The Bullmastiff needs to have the bone structure to support its weight. Ch. Nightwatch Brahms' Lullaby, owned by Cheryl Gillmore

In subsequent classes you may see a dog or dogs that appeared in earlier classes. It is wise to have 'seen' dogs, as these are termed, placed on the right-hand side of the ring. After you have examined and moved all the new dogs, ask these exhibitor(s) to join on the end of the line. Your steward will tell you if you placed the dog(s) before and in what position, or if they were unplaced. In large shows where repeat entries are usual, it is very important that your steward can give you this information about seen dogs and their placings.

While you are judging you are in charge of the ring. No one is allowed in the ring except yourself, the steward or stewards and the exhibitors. Photographers must not be allowed in the ring while the judging is taking place. Ringsiders are not allowed to take flash pictures while the dogs are being judged, so ask your steward to stop such behaviour.

Sometimes a small child runs into a ring, so stop the judging until the parent has retrieved it. If you are half way through watching a dog move, start again, as it is unfair to the exhibitor if their dog does not receive an uninterrupted examination.

Do not allow dogs to lie inside the ring at the feet of those seated at the ringside. No dog may be in the ring unless it is entered for that class. Apart from that, long tails and legs can get trodden on, exhibitors can trip over supine canines, and the exhibits may be inattentive to the job in hand if they spy a stranger in their midst. Ask your steward to get the dog removed before you continue judging.

You may be offered coffee or tea while judging an entry that is to take some time, but it is not allowed to have intoxicating beverages on the judge's table. In the old days the male judges were often seen quaffing a pint in the ring, and they also smoked while judging, but such behaviour is no longer tolerated. If you accept the offer of a hot drink, consume it between classes.

The stewards

The success or otherwise of any dog show depends largely on the experience of the stewards.

Always remember that stewards are unpaid volunteers, giving their time and expertise for the benefit of the exhibitors and judges. Good stewards who really know their job can be of immense help to any judge but especially to the possibly nervous newcomer.

As the older, more experienced stewards retire there is not a sufficient number of dedicated younger people willing to come forward to fill the vacant places, as so many either want to exhibit or to judge. However, it is a most worthwhile job and intending judges would do well to serve their time as stewards before they contemplate judging. Then they will have a good idea of the pitfalls and pleasures that await them when they finally pin on a judge's badge.

Sometimes you will be asked by the secretary if you wish to bring a steward with you. Personally, I think it wise to ask the secretary to supply the steward because the ringside might think you are asking for guidance if you are seen chatting during the judging to the friend you have brought.

Look for an alert expression.Dalmatian Ch. Washakie Indian Summer, owned by Mrs K Goff, poses for the camera.

The steward is there to help you in all particulars and not to dictate to you although, if very experienced, he may make a valid suggestion if he thinks you are heading in the wrong direction!

Do not get over-bossy in your ring. Let the stewards do their job and you concentrate on yours.

Politeness costs nothing. Friends who steward regularly often complain that many judges, both new and established, have been rude. This is unforgivable. We are all there in the same cause, the betterment of the pedigree dog, and it is easier if we get along together in a pleasant and cheerful way.

Chapter Four

A Look at the Standards

The relative merits of dogs at a show depend partly on the description of the breed compiled, usually in the past, by a body of men who were given credit at the time for possessing special knowledge of the breed.This description is authorised by one of the specialist clubs and comes to be called 'The Standard of the Breed'.

William McCandlish

The standards of the breeds established in the United Kingdom for many years all came about in the way described by Mr McCandlish. When foreign breeds arrived they brought their own standards with them, and it was not the province of dog people in Britain to tell the foreign breeders how their breeds should look or be judged. We took and used their standards as a matter of fact and courtesy.

Where there was more than one breed club, arguments over standards frequently arose between the clubs, as they did also between the top breeders of the day, especially over the merits or demerits of a particular point in the standard. Many of these battles were fought out in the dog press. An example of this is well illustrated by the furious debate that took place over whether or not the Clumber Spaniel eye should show 'haw'. Dozens of letters from most of the parties involved, for or against, were printed in the dog press for nearly a year.

Today there can be no such wide and useful discussion conducted in the knowledge that the breeders themselves will come to a decision that will be accepted by those in the breed as being best for that breed. The Kennel Club now owns the standards and no point can be altered except when the standards are revised by The Kennel Club, usually after some consultation with the breed clubs, or unless undue pressure is exerted. However, although well-argued by those in a breed, this is seldom successful.

When standards were owned by the breed clubs themselves, they were revised, altered or added to at frequent intervals. It is interesting, however, to study a breed standard together with photographs of specimens of that breed at the time. Many standards were altered to include characteristics that appeared in dogs then being shown by people who were influential in the breed. Whilst many of the characteristics added into the standards were of benefit to the breed in question, some were not, and led to trouble for the breed in later years. Perhaps this is why The Kennel Club decided to take the standards under its own control.

Boxer Ch. Freedom Fighter for Rayfos, owned by Mr Greenway.

In 1982 the last Kennel Club revision of the standards was undertaken in collaboration with the breed clubs and it was decided that all standards should be brought up to date. Old fashioned language was cut out, descriptions pruned and modern wording used in place of the older and often more descriptive terms.

It can truly be said that a 'standard' is a collection of words that means something different to everyone who reads it. Some standards today, however, are so short and bare that the would-be judge has great difficulty in picturing the breed described.

There are references that can puzzle the novice judge. For example, how do you define 'medium', a word used time and time again? Unless you know the normal and abnormal of a breed, you cannot define what 'medium' actually means. Some descriptions are so obscure that they have to be read several times before they make sense. Here are two examples: 'legs set moderately wide on line with point of shoulders', and 'from stifle to hock, in line with the extension of the upper neck line'. There is one breed where the description of the head calls for the skull to be longer than the muzzle, but the last line says, 'muzzle fairly long'!

It is these anomalies in the standards that makes it imperative for both established and new judges to study the living specimens of their breeds very carefully, so that the printed word and the animal can be made to relate one to the other. To rely solely on learning the standard of your breed parrot fashion will not make you a good judge. Standards are there as blueprints, guides to go by, not Holy Writ, so that varying types of the same breed can be accommodated within them.

Many specialist clubs now publish the standard of their breed with good line drawings and these are of immense help to judges. I urge those of you who are lucky enough to be concerned with, and hoping to judge, a breed where the breed club publishes such a standard, to get one and study it at every opportunity.

As a new judge taking on your breed for the first time, you should not only have owned and exhibited the breed but also have bred one or two litters. You should have a working knowledge of what the standard means and how to apply it. Hopefully, you have built up a small library of books, old and new, from which you have learned the particular points of your breed which you can then relate to the general information in this book. Search the stands selling old books and magazines at dog shows, and as often as you can buy copies of the Annuals issued by the two dog papers each Christmas. In these you may find photographs of the ancestors of your dogs and of the dogs you will be judging. It is essential to know what went before in your breed if you are to know how to judge it and take it forward.

Aspiring judges need not only to read about and study their breed, but to be in constant contact with it, not just through their own dogs but those of others. Lose no opportunity to visit other kennels, look at puppies and adults, and discuss the breed with like-minded people.

When exhibiting, sit at the ringside when your class is finished and really watch the dogs, preferably with a copy of the standard in your hand. Study it in relation to the animals present. To rush off home once your dog's class is over is no way to learn about your breed, and certainly will not make you a fit and proper person to undertake the onerous position of breed judge.

Ch. Valken Downtown Boy. Good conformation: a Wire Fox Terrier 'standing'. Note the deep chest, long powerful thighs and well set–on tail.

Difficulties in interpreting the standards

There are two items common to all standards. The first is headed Faults: *Any departure from the foregoing point should be considered a fault and the seriousness with which the fault should be regarded should be in exact proportion to its degree.*

Points of the dog

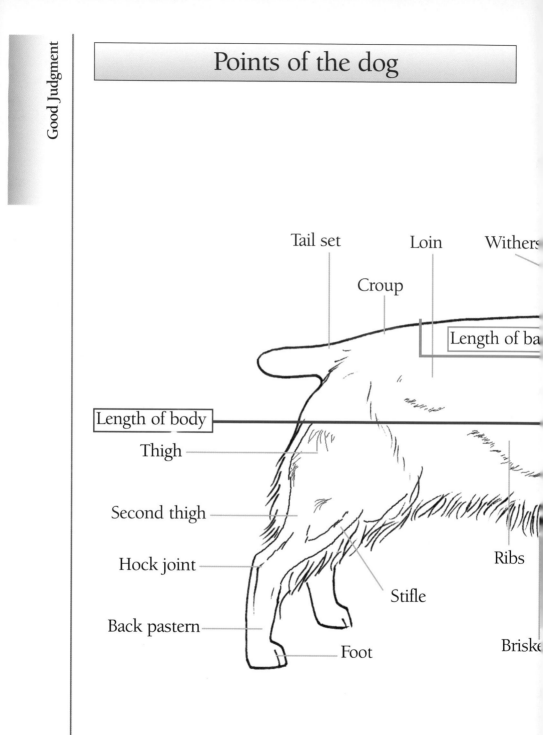

Tail set

Loin

Withers

Croup

Length of ba

Length of body

Thigh

Second thigh

Hock joint

Back pastern

Stifle

Ribs

Foot

Briske

Points of the dog

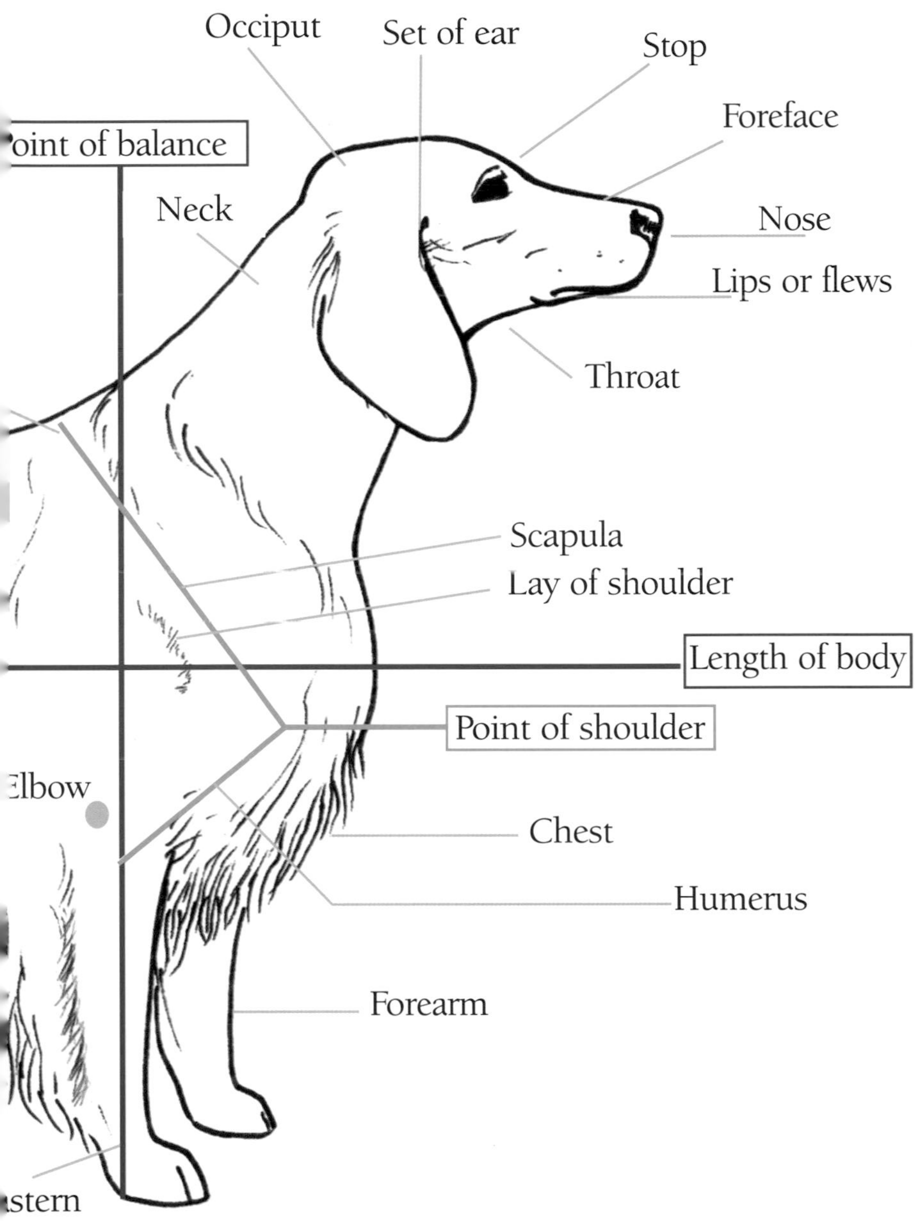

Occiput   Set of ear   Stop

Foreface

Point of balance

Neck

Nose

Lips or flews

Throat

Scapula
Lay of shoulder

Length of body

Point of shoulder

Elbow

Chest

Humerus

Forearm

Pastern

Skeleton and muscle structure

Muscle structure

1 Levator nasolabial muscle
2 Zygomaticus muscle
3 Scutularis muscle
4 Brachiocephalic muscle
5 Trapezius muscle
6 Latissimus dorsi muscle
7 Sartorius muscle
8 Gluteal muscles
9 Semitendinosus muscle
10 Quadriceps femorus muscle
11 Semimembranosus muscle
12 Gastrocnemus muscle

13 Digital flexor muscle
14 Tibialis anterior muscle
15 Abdominal muscle
16 Pectoral muscle
17 Extensor carpi ulnaris muscle
18 Flexor carpi radialis muscle
19 Extensor carpi radialis muscle
20 Triceps muscles
21 Deltoid muscles
22 Sterno-thyroid muscle
23 Masseter muscle

Skeleton and muscle structure

Skeleton and muscle structure

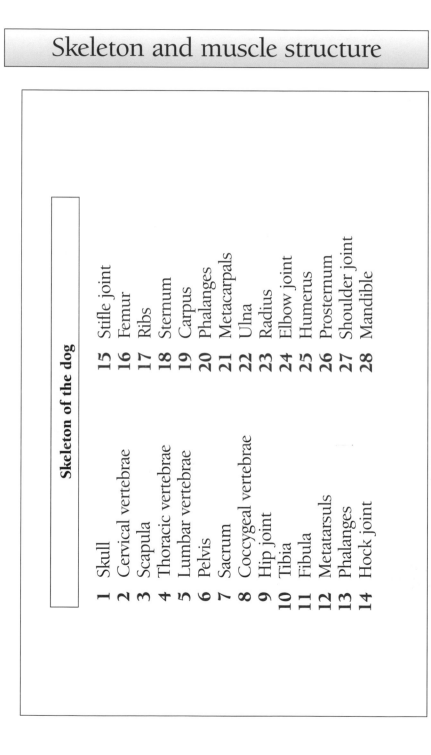

Skeleton of the dog

1 Skull
2 Cervical vertebrae
3 Scapula
4 Thoracic vertebrae
5 Lumbar vertebrae
6 Pelvis
7 Sacrum
8 Coccygeal vertebrae
9 Hip joint
10 Tibia
11 Fibula
12 Metatarsuls
13 Phalanges
14 Hock joint

15 Stifle joint
16 Femur
17 Ribs
18 Sternum
19 Carpus
20 Phalanges
21 Metacarpals
22 Ulna
23 Radius
24 Elbow joint
25 Humerus
26 Prosternum
27 Shoulder joint
28 Mandible

Skeleton and muscle structure

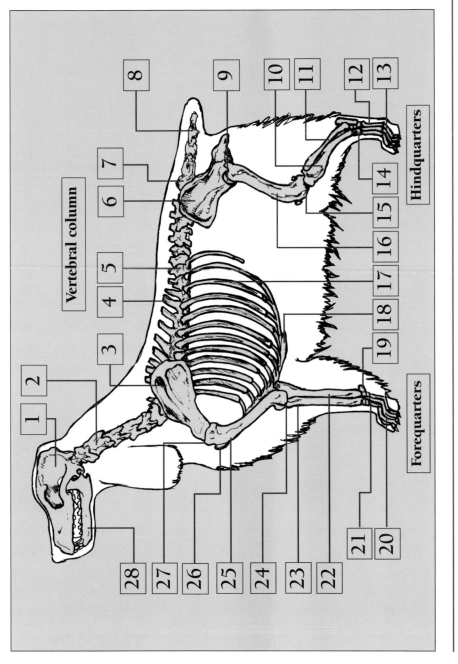

Vertebral column

Hindquarters

Forequarters

This is rather a clumsy way of saying that bad faults should be heavily penalised and lesser faults regarded more kindly. Perhaps if it read 'seriousness with which the fault *is* regarded' instead of 'should', it would make more sense to the average reader.

The second clause reads: *Note. Male animals should have two apparently normal testicles fully descended into the scrotum.*

When judging pedigree dogs it has always been with an eye to breeding better dogs in the next generation, so this note appears to be essential. This was so until the 1990s, when The Kennel Club decided that neuters of both sexes could be shown. Some of these operations are carried out for medical reasons on dogs and bitches that have already produced stock. In these cases one can understand the reason for continuing to show the animals. However, more and more frequently, some neuters that have never bred anything are finding their way into the ring.

You, the judge, find you have a dog before you with no testicles. You do not know why the dog has been neutered. The question that springs to mind is 'was he a monorchid with just one testicle descended?' Some people believe that monorchidism can run in families. If you place this dog highly and he has an entire brother, that dog might be used at stud on the strength of his sibling's wins and possibly pass the monorchid gene down to the resulting generations.

It is entirely possible that the 'neuter' is in fact a cryptorchid, that is, neither testicle had descended. It is impossible for a judge to tell whether a dog has been neutered or whether he never had testicles in the first place.

In the matter of the entire male you are caught between a rock and a hard place. The Kennel Club states that all judges should adhere to the standards. The standards call for an entire dog, yet The Kennel Club says neuter males may be shown. I do not intend to give any guidance to readers on how to act should they encounter this problem in the ring. Everyone has their own ideas on the subject, and it is presumed that new judges are capable of making up their own minds and can deal with the situation in a sensible manner.

**Ch. Dorelove Jimmy Mac, a Griffon Bruxellois, owned and
bred by Mr and Mrs N Swan**

Exhibitors showing neuters are supposed to produce a certificate from a veterinary surgeon stating the reasons for the operation, and also permission to show from The Kennel Club. Any certificates brought into the ring must be scrutinised by your steward as they should bear the registered name of the dog which you, as the judge, are not supposed to be aware of before you have judged the animal.

Bitches often have to be spayed owing to troubles with the uterus, while some are neutered to make them into easy-care pets for people unable, for whatever reason, to look after them during their twice-yearly seasons. Neuter bitches, unless carefully fed, put on excess weight and the large majority show an increase in hair growth.

It is not unusual nowadays for show bitches in coated breeds to be spayed so that they grow better furnishings and therefore have an advantage over the entire bitch. Judges of coated breeds should take this into consideration when one bitch in a class looks over-coated beside the others.

Many breed standards call for characteristics that are impossible to assess in the ring. These come under three headings: General Appearance, Characteristics and Temperament.

How are you to know if a dog is intelligent and has endurance unless you have lived with it? How do you know that the dog before you is obedient and easy to train, or enduring and faithful, or that it is a versatile working dog, capable of guarding, is outgoing, and so on? Well, you cannot know, and one can only conclude that such remarks were put in standards as a guide to people wanting to know about a breed before buying one, and not as a guide to the judge.

You can, however, gauge whether a dog is built for speed, likely to be useful as a dog for work, or able to go to ground. The first has the lines that tell the story, the second is well built and boned with a weatherproof coat, and the third can be spanned behind the shoulders by your two hands. These are only rough guides, for you cannot know if the dogs actually are suited temperamentally for any of these jobs, nor could you know until the dogs are put in a situation where they are called on to demonstrate the fact.

Withholding

This seems an appropriate place to discuss this thorny subject.

Withholding a prize occurs mainly when there is a very small entry in a class. If you are faced with a dog or bitch that fails in many essentials, such as very over- or under-sized, lacking in type or grossly unsound, showing aggressive temperament or obviously suffering from some illness, you may feel that the only course open to you is to withhold. Although prizes are occasionally withheld at open show level, withholding occurs more often at championship shows.

Some judges maintain that to give first prize to a poor specimen in a class that will qualify it for Crufts or earn it a place in the Stud Book does no good to the breed, while others say that the judge should not take such things into consideration. Others argue that prizes are there to be won and should be handed out no matter how sub-standard the dogs are.

At the start of your judging career, you have to decide for yourself how you are going to handle this situation. You will be faced with it at some time, and it will help if you have given it some thought and decided how you are going to proceed when the occasion arises.

Before you withhold at an open show you must be quite satisfied in your own mind that the dog is of such poor quality and so totally lacking in characteristics of the breed that it is quite unworthy to win an award. The basic rule is that if you withhold both 1st and 2nd prizes, other prizes must also be withheld.

Many judges are afraid to withhold, aware of the wrath that will descend on their heads from the owner and his friends. Some are afraid that if they withhold they will not be asked to judge again. To those at the start of a judging career I would say, never compromise your principles for the sake of popularity.

For your own information I suggest that you obtain from The Kennel Club not only their booklet, *Guide for Judges*, but also a copy of show rules and regulations. Also subscribe to the monthly *Kennel Gazette*, where all rule changes are printed, so that you are up-to-date on what you can and cannot do.

It is as well to bear in mind that all breeds were evolved originally for a specific purpose, such as for draught work, as guards, shepherding, as gundogs, and so on. While many specimens of these breeds no longer do the work for which they were bred, this does not mean that they should not be constructed and conditioned so that they could do those tasks should they be asked. The design of each breed to do its alloted task formed the basis of the standard for the breed. In my view, no one person can know the finer points of every breed and it would be an impudence to pretend one does.

This book does not tell you how to judge all the various breeds. It is a general book aimed at helping the newer judge to understand the principles and practice of judging and to appreciate the form and functions of the dog.

Chapter Five

Judging the Whole Dog

When a judge judges dogs as a whole, and not as an accumulation of points, he will make his decisions on the general appearance of the exhibits after he has carefully handled them to assure himself there are no hidden defects, and is satisfied, after close scrutiny, that the dog is as good as he appears to be.

William McCandlish

Like people in all walks of life today, dog judges are bombarded with slogans. One is 'you must not fault judge', though what judging is about except putting up the dog with the least number of faults, I am not sure! Another is 'you must judge the whole dog'. When you have a dog in front of you it is rather difficult to judge odd bits of it, but occasionally judges do just that, especially if they have a particular interest in some aspect of their breed, for example, heads, coats, eye colour, ear set and so on. No doubt, this is what has given rise to that slogan.

The 'whole dog', as I see it, is a balanced animal, correctly constructed with good proportions, well muscled, conditioned and coated, that moves soundly and carries good breed type. It is not often that you find one dog which has all these things, but judging is about finding as many of them in one specimen as you can and not just standing in the ring choosing a line up. There is a great deal of difference between 'judging' and 'choosing'.

'Balance' is the key word when assessing dogs. Firstly, the dog should stand on four good legs and feet and this goes equally for a Chihuahua or a Great Dane. The displacement of weight must be equal between the front and rear ends, so the dog stands square using all of the pads of the feet. The shoulders should be correctly developed for the breed, and the neck fit neatly and be strong and well muscled in order to hold the head at the correct angle. The term often used by judges is that the dog is 'standing over its ground'.

St Bernard Ch. Meadowmead Helena   **Photograph by Carol Ann Johnson**

This is where the term 'fit the frame' comes in. Each breed has a different frame; for instance, French Bulldogs and German Shepherd Dogs have very different frames, but they do each have a frame. If you have a natural 'eye', you will spot immediately which dog 'fits the frame'. To educate your eye so that it can comprehend line, form and balance at a glance, use the artist's trick of measuring perspective.

Take a pencil in your hand and stand away from the dog that is held steady in profile. Shut one eye and hold the pencil between thumb and fingers half way up its length, in an upright position between you and the dog. Take the top of the withers as your focal

Find out what has gone before. Clumber Spaniel Ch. Auckwear Ripper, 1936, courtesy of Thomas Fall

point, as this is the point of balance for all animals, and you will get the idea of height, and then turn the pencil sideways to get the length. Do this several times with different dogs and you soon will be able to see the balanced dog, the one that 'fits the frame'.

To achieve perfect balance the dog must be structurally sound and the structure held together with good muscle. All parts of the dog must be properly developed for the breed in question. Bone must be in balance with the body. For instance, a large-headed, heavy-bodied dog like the Clumber Spaniel or St Bernard will be quite unbalanced if the bone is poorly developed. Heavy breeds with poor bone usually have dips in their top lines as the weight of the body is not properly supported, and usually this is accompanied by slack or bowed shoulders and cow hocks. Breeds with long bodies, such as the Dachshund and Basset Hound, need to be well-conditioned and exercised to develop muscles in shoulders, hind legs and, especially, backs if they are to present the desired outline and move strongly.

Toy dogs should be viewed as dogs first and toys second. They should be as well-constructed and muscled as their larger brethren if they are to live long and healthy lives.

Judging is as much about putting up dogs least likely to suffer health problems as about type and quality. No standard has ever called for a sickly dog, however beautiful, neither can I recall a standard that asks for a typey cripple.

Much damage was done many years ago when a very well-known judge delivered himself of the pronouncement that he would 'place type before soundness as any old mongrel can be sound'. This, because someone of experience and influence uttered the words, has been taken up as a battle cry by those who wish to be regarded as well informed. The end result has been many, many more poorly-constructed and badly-moving dogs entering the rings. You, as a new judge, need to be very careful of slogans that suddenly come to the fore.

Weigh up what the outcome would be if everyone followed the edicts and fads of a few, however well known and influential. In the world of livestock breeding some pronouncements can have lasting and harmful effects.

Coats may cause you a few anxious moments. Everyone has their own idea about how much to penalise an out-of-coat dog. Some years ago, two famous dog breeders and judges wrote about judging their breed. One said, 'I would never put up a dog that was in less than full coat.' The other wrote, 'I do not mind if a very good specimen is out of coat, coats will grow but good structure is always there.' I agree with the second judge, and if you have a really top-class dog that is a bit lacking in furnishings on the day, do not be afraid to place it provided the colour and texture is right.

Sometimes you will have a dog that thoroughly puzzles you – you like it and yet you do not like it. Something is wrong, but you cannot

Ear shapes and carriages

1. Triangular erect: Belgian Shepherd Dog.

2. Triangular drop: Pyrenean Mountain Dog.

3. Prick ear: Norwich Terrier.

4. Rose ear:
   Italian
   Greyhound.

5. Vine leaf:
   Clumber Spaniel.

6. Lobular:
   Cocker Spaniel.

Ear shapes and carriages

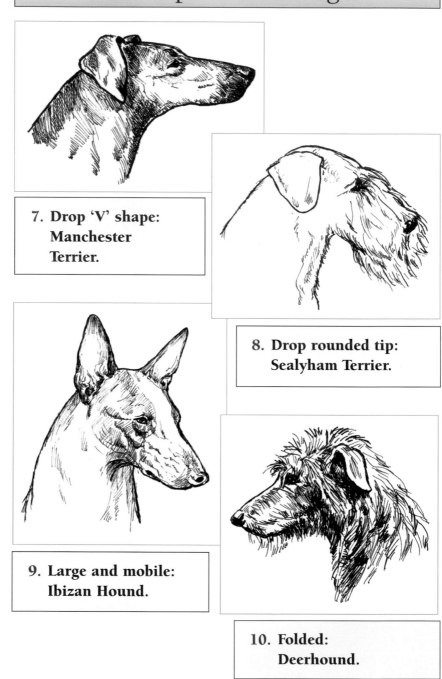

7. Drop 'V' shape: Manchester Terrier.

8. Drop rounded tip: Sealyham Terrier.

9. Large and mobile: Ibizan Hound.

10. Folded: Deerhound.

11. Bat ear:
    French Bulldog.

12. Semi-erect:
    Rough Collie.

13. Candle flame:
    English Toy Terrier.

14. Butterfly:
    Papillion.

put your finger on it. It is best to trust to your instincts if they tell you the dog is not quite right, better to place it lower than higher in a class or even leave it on the side lines. The old judges used to say, 'When in doubt, leave it out.' It is a very good motto to follow.

Judging the whole puppy

Keep a very open mind when judging puppies. First, your approach to them must be friendly. Always speak to them and try to reassure them, as some are very overawed by the proceedings. Many puppies are only just six months old when they are brought into the ring, some have no manners at all, others are very self possessed, some may have been taken very young to handling classes and may already be blasé about the whole thing, or may have been put off completely. Puppies, as well as adults, should always be handled firmly but kindly. Do not put 'fairy fingers' on a dog's back, especially not a puppy's, as it is liable to become frightened. A firm, but not hard, hand is what is needed. Do handle puppies sympathetically, never be rough, and when examining a male pup for entirety, do not grab the testicles but feel gently. I have seen rough judges who have put puppies off showing for life.

If the puppy has not learned about having its mouth examined, get the owner to lift its lips.

Very mature puppies have a tendency to go coarse in adulthood; very undersized puppies rarely make the required size for the breed; while puppies already at the adult height may have grown fast and may not be too big when fully mature but, of course, may go on growing and become oversized. You need to think about size, and balance this with the puppy's other characteristics when making your line-up.

Puppies with poor bone rarely improve in this area.

Heads on various breeds do alter as the pups grow.

Puppies that are unsound on the move very rarely improve, so look for a well-built puppy that stands true and can move easily although it may not be fully tightened in movement. You may never know how the puppy you are judging will turn out, so do not be extreme in your description but, if you are really excited about its future prospects, qualify your critique with the word 'promising' or 'should make up well'.

The majority of puppies are happy with their world and settle in the ring but some may be shy and need some coaxing. It is worth spending a little extra time to give the babies every chance to show themselves off and gain much-needed experience.

Maturity changes the puppy considerably, so do not try too hard to look into the future. Try to look at the puppy as an unfinished article to be judged on its virtues on the day.

Who can tell if this young Westie will grow into a show champion?

Dealing with the blemishes

As your judging career unfolds you will be constantly amazed at the number of dogs shown bearing the scars of repairs.

In recent years The Kennel Club has granted 'permission to show' to dogs that have undergone a variety of operations to eyes, teeth, stifles and so on, which hitherto has rendered the dog unsuitable for exhibition.

Below are some examples of the sorts of dogs which will come under you:

1. Dogs which have permission to be shown with repaired cruciate ligaments said to have been caused by an injury. The cruciate ligaments are two strong ligaments in the stifle joint which prevent any possibility of over-extension of the joint. This means they prevent slipping stifles which are found in a number of breeds where the cruciate ligament is not working as it should. It is quite easy to tell if a dog has had such an operation as there is a thickening of the area round the stifle joint. Movement is not affected to any extent, although you may see a deviation as you watch the cadence, that is, the rhythm as the dog places its feet down. Count the steps as the dog trots, one, two, three, four, and you may find the rhythm breaks slightly as the dog puts one of its hind legs on the ground.

2. Dogs that have had repairs to their eyelids, that is, they have been operated on either for Entropion (turning in of the lids) or Ectropion (turning out of the lids). Veterinary surgery is done so skilfully nowadays that in many cases there is no scar of any sort to show that the dog has had this type of operation. Most exhibitors hope such operations do not show, but there is always the exception, and once a lady put her dog on the table for me to examine and declared in ringing and triumphant tones, 'He's had his eyes done!'

3. Dogs that have had dental surgery. If the exhibitor tells you the teeth have been extracted, you have no means of knowing if this statement is true or whether the dog never had the missing teeth in the first place. Sometimes where much surgery has been done in the mouth, the line of the lips and shape of the face alters, thereby giving an untrue picture of the desired head.

4. Frequently, people apply for permission to show when the dog

has had one or two toes amputated. The loss of any toes is bound to affect movement to some extent, as the dog cannot stand square and so cannot move off all four feet with the same pressure.

5. Many long-tailed breeds kept indoors suffer damage from banging the tail against furniture and metal objects in the home. They also get their tails shut in car doors. Permission to show is granted to various long-tailed breeds which have suffered such injuries and have had to have the tail shortened. However, the dog with a shortened tail does not exhibit any signs of discomfort or difference in movement although the overall outline will be affected.

Many people show their dogs with lesser blemishes. This did not happen in the past, as exhibitors kept the dog at home until it was whole again.

Chinese Crested Ch. Debrita Defiant 'standing over his ground'.

Eye shapes

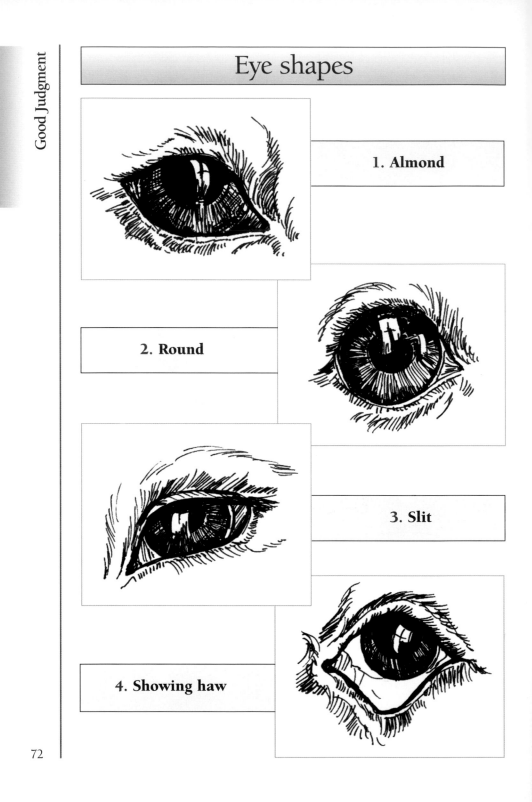

1. Almond

2. Round

3. Slit

4. Showing haw

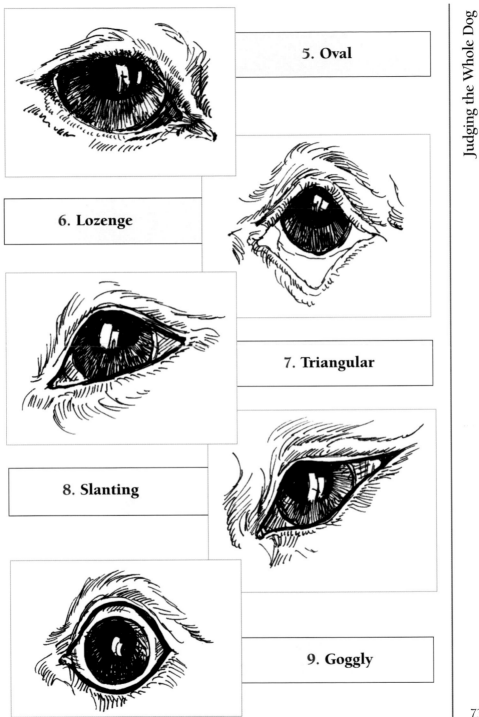

5. Oval

6. Lozenge

7. Triangular

8. Slanting

9. Goggly

Sh. Ch. Jennaline Kentish Krumpet, a German Shorthaired Pointer, owned by Mrs Jennings, has clean, well-laid shoulders, well-constructed hind quarters and firm, well-boned legs.

6. A dog that has torn itself on a barbed wire fence and been sewn up by the veterinary surgeon a day or so before will not only have a raw wound with stitches, but some of its coat will have been shaved off to facilitate the repair. One of its legs will also be shaved where the injections have been administered.

7. Dogs that have had some kind of skin infection are shown with bald patches.

8. Dogs that have been stung by wasps or bees come with swollen faces.

9. Dogs come bearing scars of recent fights, or burn marks where they have got too close to the fire or, in lesser cases, singed hair which alters the required shade of the coat. Exhibitors are in such a hurry

to show their dogs that they fail to appreciate when the animal is not in show condition. If, however, you are judging one of the terrier breeds designated as 'working', such as Border Terrier or Parson Jack Russell, you should never penalise 'honourable' scars incurred as a result of their work.

At some time during your early judging career you are bound to come up against one or more of these problems, and it is as well to think about how you intend to deal with them when they arise. It is not my province to tell you how to behave in any these circumstances, as everyone has their own standards and must abide by them. However, bearing in mind that your job is to judge the 'whole dog', any deviation must be classed as a failing and considered in context with the dog's virtues when you choose a line-up.

Ch. Michandy Va La is a Miniature Poodle owned by Jackie Kitchener. The novice judge needs to make sure that, in a coated or trimmed breed, the shoulder is well laid and the legs come 'out of the coat' in the right place.

Chapter Six

Movement

The factor of first importance in all dogs is soundness. However wonderful a dog's head or any other part may be, it is of no value in a show ring unless there are sound legs and constitution to carry the wonderful head about the world.

William McCandlish

Movement, locomotion, gait, call it what you will, is of prime importance when judging dogs of any breed and is tied up inextricably with correct structure, musculature and general fitness. If a dog cannot move easily and comfortably, it is unlikely to be a durable specimen and has little chance of living a long and active life.

No dog can move correctly unless its balance is right. The easiest way to assess balance is to use a plumb line. Stand the dog square on an even surface, place the line on its withers, and the weighted end should fall down straight behind the front leg through the elbow joint. The withers are the point of balance in the dog, and wrong proportions here throw the rest off balance.

I am not suggesting that you should adopt this practice in the ring, but you should use this method on your own and other people's dogs as part of the learning process. Afterwards, when you are judging you can spot the dogs with correct shoulders without the benefit of the plumb line.

A dog's legs move in parallel fashion, the hind legs being in line with the front legs. The movement at the trot should be of an even cadence, and the dog should 'track up', that is, not leave the back legs behind on the move. It should also not 'over reach', which is when the hind leg comes so far forward at the trot as to hit the foreleg or even land before it.

You, the judge, will find many deviations from the norm: poorly developed muscle, insufficient bone to support the weight of the body, overlong loins, loaded shoulders, upright shoulders, narrow

The plumb line is a thin cord fastened to a lump of lead or brass. Stand the dog square and place the cord on the withers, allowing the weighted end to fall to ground level. If the dog's shoulders are correct, as they are in this photograph, the plumb will make a line through the elbow and down the back of the front leg. If the line does not fall at this angle then the shoulder is not well laid.

quarters, straight stifles, slipping stifles, slipping hock joint, bowed hocks, out at shoulder, out at elbow, tied in at the elbows, poor feet. All these affect movement.

Before you go over each dog individually, send the whole class around the ring. You will soon learn to spot the dogs with faults in conformation and movement. In individual examinations, it is important either to move the dog in a triangle, to see the front, side and rear movement, or to move the dog twice in a straight line, stepping to one side to see the profile on the second move.

The dog's propulsion comes from behind. The saying goes, 'The engine of the dog is situated at the rear', so well-developed quarters and correct proportions to the hind leg are essential to produce the rear drive that propels the dog forward, enabling the shoulders to engage and allowing the front movement to come into play.

A dog 'plaiting' (crossing its front legs) on the move indicates lack of drive from the rear. The dog is actually pulling itself along by its shoulders.

A dog whose natural pace is the trot tends to 'go into the ground' if it has upright shoulders and straight stifles.

In the hound breeds, whose natural gait is the gallop, you will find that the trot is lighter and more contained but still forward going.

Cow hocks, when the hock joints point towards each other, or bowed hocks, when the hock joints turn outwards, account for some bad rear movement.

Overlong loins are usually weak; the dog has difficulty controlling its quarters and moves with a twisting gait, never being able to get the desired drive.

Over-fat dogs tend to have loaded shoulders. The fat settles on the muscles of the shoulder and gives a heaviness in front which causes the dog to roll slightly. Slack shoulders usually indicate poor development of the pectoral muscles that attach shoulder bones to the rib cage.

Weak pasterns cause the feet to turn outwards and the dog tends to roll in movement.

Narrow quarters mean the dog has a 'tied-in' movement, that is, the legs appear to be going up and down instead of forward. The same is true of tied-in elbows and in neither case can the dog move easily.

Poor feet can cause poor movement. Flat-footed dogs (walking on the back pad) have heavy movement. Dogs with upright shoulders tend to walk and stand with more pressure on the front pads so it is worth looking at the feet and studying where the pressure comes. The foot should show even wear, which means that the dog is balanced and using its feet correctly.

This long-legged Irish Water Spaniel displays good ground-covering movement using all its body and placing the feet correctly, neither over-reaching nor moving on too short a stride.

Ideally the dog should have the width of quarters to match the rib cage, the two joined by a strong loin. This is true of every breed, no matter what its size or shape, and makes for correct balance.

Muscle tone has deteriorated greatly in all breeds since I started my judging career, and this is due to the change in how the show dog is kept. In the past, most show dogs were kennelled in runs so they could move around, play and exercise all day if they so wished. Today, the large majority are house dogs which lie around in over-heated, airless conditions. More and more parks and open spaces are banned to dogs, lessening the chance to give them a good, free gallop. Only those who live far out in the country or adjacent to mountains and moorlands can be said to have ideal exercising country. Roads are so dangerous that it is no longer possible to exercise dogs beside a bicycle.

Add to this the cage revolution. In America, the professional handlers use cages in their motorised trailers to confine the dogs during their continuous journeying around the show circuit. Cages are also used to hold the dogs at the shows, as few shows in the United States are benched.

Cages have caught on here in a big way; they are convenient to have in an estate or hatchback, fit neatly into the corner of the room so the dog can be shut away and not be a nuisance, and are invaluable to owners of coated breeds who shut up their dogs for long hours so their coiffures do not get rumpled!

All this has meant a deterioration in muscle tone. As a judge, you will quickly spot the dogs that lead normal, free lives by the muscle found in shoulders, neck, back, quarters and thighs. There are many fat dogs who puff around the ring, dogs with slack shoulders, dogs with no discernable drive from the rear. You will find that only a minority of dogs are really in a tip-top physical state, well-fleshed with no excess blubber, well-developed taut muscles, and sound ground-covering movement. However good the original skeleton, without proper muscling it cannot be made to work correctly.

Good feet are necessary for all breeds. Not only must the foot be the right shape for the breed, it must be strong, tight and well padded. It is not unusual to find a lame dog in the class. Many and wonderful are the excuses for a lame dog, such as these I have heard:

'Well, I know he was lame yesterday, but I thought he would be all right today.'

'He jumped out of the car window, but I did not think he had hurt himself.'

'He's had an operation on his foot, but the vet said he would be able to walk.'

The dog must be able to do the job it was bred for. Sh. Ch. Quettadene Discretion, a Cocker Spaniel owned by Mrs Lester, is fit and alert.

81

However the most common remark is, 'Is he really? Well, I didn't notice!'

If the owner of the lame dog does not wish to leave the ring, then he may stay in, but whether or not you care to place the dog depends on the number and quality of the sound exhibits. You will have to decide there and then whether to place a lame dog, balancing all its other qualities against the lameness.

If the dog is hopping lame and you suggest (never order) that the dog is withdrawn from the class, the handler may ask for a veterinary opinion. This is a fairly rare request in dog showing, but does happen very occasionally. It can hold up proceedings indefinitely, particularly if the vet is not present but only on call. It is up to the judge to deal carefully and tactfully with exhibitors and lame dogs.

When assessing the action of many of the giant breeds you may find yourself greatly hindered by the handler. Some handlers are far too small to do justice to such big dogs, some are patently not strong enough, and some too infirm to give the dog a sporting chance on the move. Other handlers are big enough, young enough and strong enough, but seek to dominate the exhibit, holding it up on a very tight lead and pulling the head back so that the shoulders open and spoil the front and the back hollows. This alters the outline both in repose and on the move. The dog is being so tightly controlled that it is unable to use itself in the correct manner.

Many exhibitors now consider that the only way to show a dog is by stringing it up as tightly as possible, apparently unaware that this ruins the outline and makes it impossible for the dog to move at a suitable pace for its breed. Some handlers use this method so excessively that the dog's forefeet never touch the floor! Some exhibitors string their dogs up so tightly that the animals appear to be choking, and gulp and gasp as they are being evaluated. You have the right to ask the exhibitor to show the dog in a more humane way.

Another bugbear nowadays is speed. Exhibitors seem to think that the faster they go, the more showy the dog. Nothing could be further from the truth. Every breed has a pace at which it moves best, but few exhibitors recognise this and continue to overpace their charges. Many a placing has been lost by the handler who pulls his dog off balance on the move, particularly when cornering. Never be afraid to ask the exhibitor to go more slowly so that you can get a better idea of the dog on the move.

Judge the toy breeds in just the same way as the larger dogs. They all have the same bone structure and musculature. Properly-constructed toys stand out in the ring, not only for their good frames and correct muscle development, but for their smart movement and bright, intelligent outlook. Do not skimp your examination of the toy breeds. You will soon learn which dogs lead normal lives and which spend their days in cages.

The Basset Hound needs to be able to move forward smoothly at a good pace when at work. This hound displays the ability to cover the ground in the correct manner.

A dog that is well constructed and muscled, and is sound and active on the move has a better chance of being of value to its breed, and also of living to a healthy old age. As judges, we have a duty to place dogs not only of good type, but also well constructed, sound animals that can live out their allotted life span in comfort.

Movement

1. **Correct forward movement. The dog is well balanced.**

2. **Hackney action. The feet are raised high in the air.**

3. **Over reaching. The hindleg is overlapping the front leg.**

4. **Pacing. Both legs on each side move in the same direction. This produces a waddling effect.**

5. Plaiting.
The dog places one
foot over the other
when moving,
indicating no rear
drive. The dog is
pulling itself along
by its shoulders.

Direction
of travel

6. This dog is pulling
away from handler
and the judge
cannot assess
movement.

Direction
of travel

7. Crabbing.
Again, assessment
of movement
cannot be made.

Chapter Seven

Judging Mouths

A judge is, for the time being, the trustee of the breed, and it may be necessary, and often is necessary, to place greater importance on some fault or feature, for the time being, than would be placed normally.

William McCandlish

At the start of your career, you should learn about the importance of teeth. Dogs, like all other animals, including humans, have teeth to enable them to chew their food and make it digestible. The internal organs can then work properly and the animal remains healthy.

Originally all the dog's teeth were there to help it survive in the wild. Eye teeth were used to catch and kill prey and tear the meat off the bones. Molars crunched the bones. Incisors were used to nibble the last of the meat from the bones, while the pre-molars softened large chunks of the meat so that it could be swallowed easily.

The domesticated dog no longer uses its teeth for these purposes, but good teeth are still needed by all dogs. Without a full or nearly full complement of teeth, they are at a disadvantage to their fellows. Judges who say that teeth do not matter are doing a great disservice to pedigree dogs, not only by passing faulty mouths but, in doing so, inhibiting the dogs' right to good health.

A full complement of teeth comprises four canine (eye) teeth, 12 incisors, 16 pre-molars and 10 molars, a total of 42. Two eye teeth are located either side of the bottom teeth, locking in front of the two upper eye teeth. There are six incisors top and bottom between the eye teeth. Four top and four bottom pre-molars are set either side of the jaw behind the eye teeth, and behind them are the 10 molars, three on each side of the upper jaw and two on each side of the bottom jaw.

The 'scissor' bite called for in a large number of breeds means that the top incisors fit neatly over the bottom incisors. Some breeds have a 'reversed scissor', where the bottom incisors fit snugly in front of and against the upper incisors. In some breeds the mouth should be 'slightly undershot'. This means that there is a small gap between the top and bottom incisors, with the bottom jaw slightly protruding. In breeds that are undershot, such as the bull breeds, the six bottom incisors should be well formed and in a straight line.

A very few breeds allow a level (or pincer) bite, where the top and bottom incisors meet together in a straight line.

You will see some very strange mouths during your judging career. Missing pre-molars are a feature of several breeds, but please do not listen to those people who tell you that a few missing pre-molars do not matter. They matter as much as any teeth.

Some dogs are born with only 40 or 41 of their full complement of teeth. This can be acceptable, but a number of missing pre-molars can point to a shortage of teeth in that breed, or line within the breed. When dogs with such faults are mated together, there is bound to be a deterioration of numbers of teeth in the following generations.

Missing pre-molars in dogs with long forefaces such as Spaniels and Setters mean that the face tends to 'fall in' at the point where the teeth are missing. Viewed from the front, the dog looks as if it is sucking in its lips, and the lack of teeth can also result in a 'down face' appearance. It is noticeable that dogs with a number of missing pre-molars have narrow underjaws and lack chin. The bottom incisors may be cramped for space and protrude outwards.

Dogs with missing incisors or eye teeth should be viewed with some suspicion but, if you ask, the exhibitor always has a variety of excuses! The dog:

'Knocked it (them) out while playing.'

'Pulled them out chewing.'

'Lost them while working.'

'Had them extracted on veterinary advice, but the dog has a "permission to show" from The Kennel Club.'

While the tale is sometimes true, very often the teeth may never have been in place!

An undershot jaw, where the lower jaw protrudes in front of the

Judging mouths: teeth

1. Scissor bite

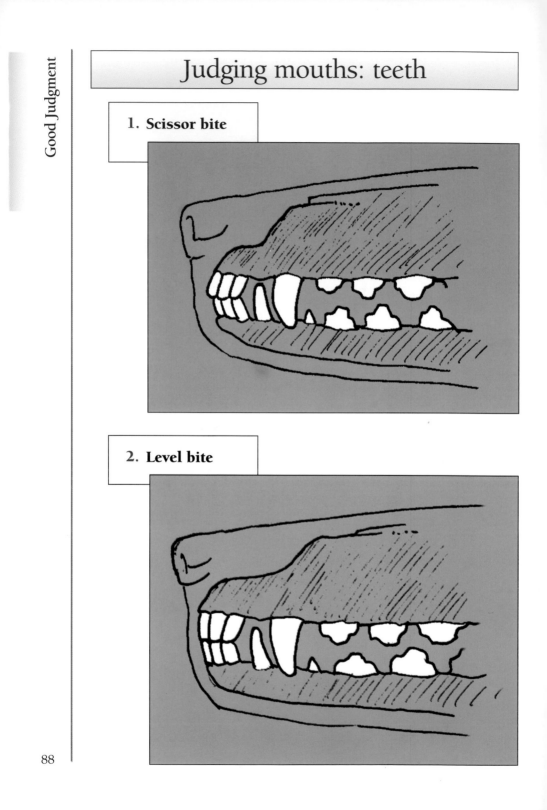

2. Level bite

3. Overshot

4. Undershot

5. Reversed scissor

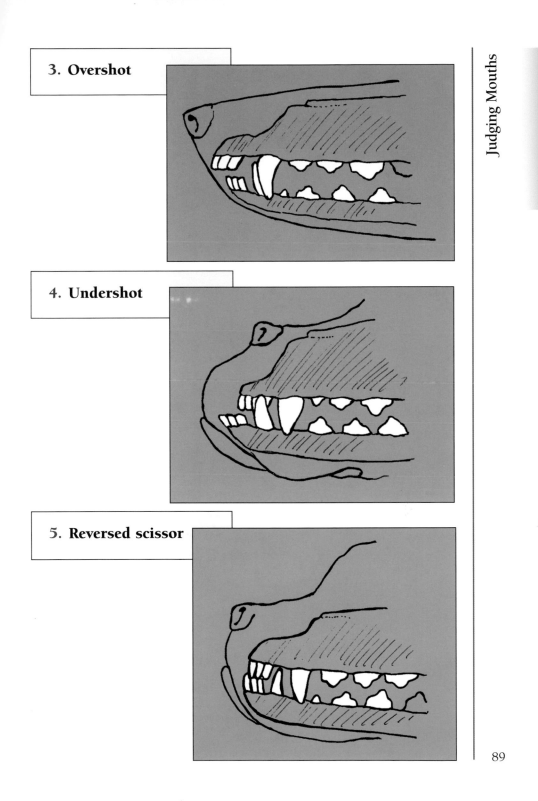

Judging mouths: jaws and teeth

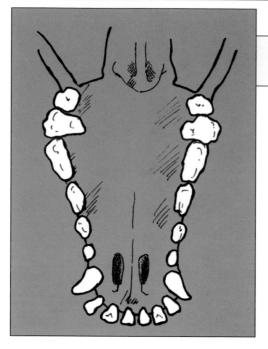

6. Upper jaw

7. Lower jaw

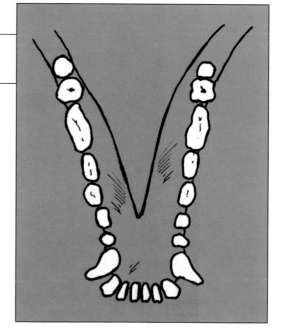

8. Correct dentition (side view)

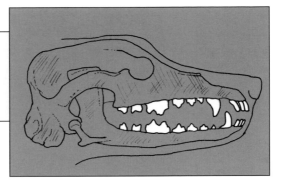

9. Correct dentition (front view)

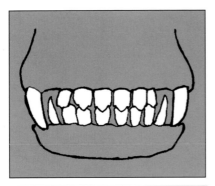

10. Crooked jaw

11. Offset or wry mouth. Dog cannot control the tongue.

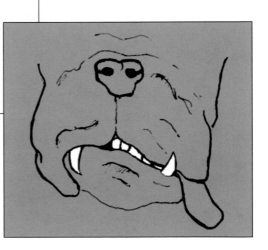

upper jaw leaving a sizeable gap between top and bottom incisors, is a fault in breeds where a scissor bite is called for. The overshot (pig) jaw is where the upper jaw protrudes considerably in front of the lower jaw. In the wry mouth, the jaws are set on a skew one to another. A pointer to this fault is that the dog's tongue tends to hang out of the mouth on one side or the other, as the jaws are so badly constructed that the tongue cannot be held in place. Wry jaws are a deformity and dogs with this fault should not be placed.

You will be faced with a variety of small problems that cannot be described as bad faults but which should be put in perspective when judging the dog as a whole. These include a twisted tooth, a tooth out of line, a double incisor (where two seem to be fused together) and double rows, where the milk teeth are still in the jaw and the second teeth have grown up around them. In quite a number of mouths you will find two centre bottom incisors set below the rest. This is another fault which could be passed on to future generations.

If you are judging two good dogs and one has a mouth failing, then the other dog should go up and the poorer exhibit placed second. If you place a male highly, even though it has a poor bite, the dog will probably be used at stud and pass the problem to his descendants.

When you progress to breeds other than your own, study the requirements for each breed's mouth in the relevant standard, as there may be something which runs counter to your experience. For example, the standard for the Pyrenean Mountain Dog reads: *although the breed should have a scissor bite, a pincer or level bite is tolerated, and the two central incisors may be set lower than the rest.*

Many dogs today are fed on soft food and never get anything to chew. This results in sore, inflamed gums, and stained, tartar-encrusted teeth. Although most people give the dogs 'toys', these are not beneficial unless chosen from those products specifically designed to help dental health.

You will probably be faced with dogs that have had various teeth removed by surgery. These operations include the extraction of molars and pre-molars, removal of a broken tooth, extraction of a fractured eye tooth, and removal of incisors. This means that the dog has an incomplete mouth, and that its face has an altered lip line and, possibly, expression.

Many breeds have a tooth formation bred into them to enable them to carry out the work for which they were evolved. The bull breeds, used in the past for bull and bear baiting, have the brachycephalic head with the underjaw longer than the upper, which forms the characteristic, immensely strong, undershot mouth that enabled them to catch and hang on to the baited animal.

Retrievers and Spaniels have large, well-developed teeth that allow them to retrieve the shot game cleanly and 'runners' with no injury. If they have small teeth, they are liable to be hard mouthed. Hound breeds, bred to chase and kill, need good, well-shaped mouths with large, strong teeth, while terriers should have strong jaws, well-developed and with large white teeth meeting in a rat-trap bite.

The Flatcoated Retriever must be able to retrieve game cleanly. Photograph by Liz Phillips

Some of the toy breeds tend to lose their teeth early, possibly due to a soft diet and a neglected cleaning programme. However, they need good teeth as much as the larger dogs so they can lead healthy lives.

Chapter Eight

Type and Quality

...before he enters the ring the judge must have a clear conception of the breed characteristics of the particular animals he is judging. These breed characteristics are commonly referred to by the name of Type.

William McCandlish

You may have been confused at times by the bandying about of the word 'type', and by people who write in their reports, 'not my type'. No dog of any breed can be described by someone as 'not their type', because the type, or standard, is a statement of the characteristics of that breed written down for all to see and immutable until altered by those in authority.

You will judge some dogs that have a lot of 'breed type', that is, they have most of the characteristics desired in that breed. Some will be 'untypical' in that they have only some of the desired characteristics, but you must not describe a dog as 'not my type' because you did not lay down the blueprint for the breed.

You will prefer one dog to another, because the various characteristics that make up the whole type in any dog will be differently distributed, and each judge lays different emphasis on different things. For instance, if you are a 'head' judge, you may be influenced by a beautiful head that is exactly to type, although the rib cage may be shorter or longer or the height does not conform to the standard. If construction and soundness are your personal concerns, you may prefer the well-made, sound moving dog of correct size whose head lacks some character. We all see type in different ways.

Type, however, is not something that you decide for yourself. In his book, William McCandlish writes:

While all dogs, indifferent and bad of a breed, must have something in common to enable them to be discerned as members of that breed, it is necessary to make certain characteristics essential if any distinction is to be drawn between good and bad breed type. There must be some selection made, but this selection should not be limited to too narrow a margin. In individual type it is the small differences that matter, but breed type is expressed more by general appearance than by detailed inspection.

This wise pronouncement asks the breed judge to look first at the overall picture of the dogs in a class and spot the ones which have the most characteristics of the breed. Then a detailed examination of each dog discovers the finer points as well as the faults.

However, Mr McCandlish warns in another chapter that no matter how much type a dog shows, that is, how many desired characteristics of the breed the dog has, it is not a viable proposition unless it is soundly made and moving correctly.

**Irish Wolfhound Ch. and Ob. Trial Ch. Superstar in Neon on Georgian Bay.
Photograph by Kevin Proud**

As the standard is a blueprint for a breed, so as a judge you must move within its framework, endeavouring to find as many of the virtues or characteristics demanded by the standard as possible in the dog you are examining. Type and soundness must go hand in hand, one never being sacrificed entirely to the other, but a balance struck between the two.

Two things help to make type in all breeds, and these are the head and the tail. The correct head for the breed sets the seal on a typical, or characteristic, specimen for without the desired head you do not have the breed. Heads may vary in quality, or eye and ear set, but the characteristic shape for that breed must be present. For example, a

One of the great examples of quality, Lhasa Apso Ch. Saxonsprings Fresno. This beautiful bitch was bred and owned by Mrs Jean Blyth and handled to her many successes at top level by Geoff Corish. Fresno will go down in history as the 'Top Dog of the Eighties'. Fresno is pictured with the Send Gold Vase after winning the Utility Group at Crufts in 1988. **Photograph by David Dalton**

Pointer should not have a head like a Spaniel, nor should a Dachshund have the head of a Beagle.

Tails are as important in type as heads. Their length, set, carriage and use determines whether the tail is typical of the breed. Setters' tails should not curve over their backs; if they do, the set as well as the carriage is uncharacteristic. Pack hounds should not have tails (called 'sterns' in hound breeds) trailing behind them, or they will have an uncharacteristic and therefore untypical outline.

Land Spaniels, Cocker, Springer and so on should have tails set and carried on a level with their backs with a fast-moving action. Any Spaniel tail that is too short or too long, or raised higher than the back and not used in the correct manner, is uncharacteristic and therefore untypical.

The length, set and carriage of the tail has a great deal to do with the overall outline, both when the dog is standing still and when it is on the move.

Quality

Quality is hard to define but is immediately apparent to the judge with eyes to see something special. Some might describe quality as a fusion of type, soundness, proportion, balance and temperament allied to presence and presentation, and maybe they are right. Perhaps it is something so intangible that it has to 'hit you in the eye', and if you have any feel for a good dog, you will not fail to recognise it. Quality is a refinement of all that is best; there is no coarseness, no crudity, no compromise.

No dog with any obvious fault, a head not entirely typical, any unsoundness of construction or movement, anything less than the best of coat texture, anything but the best of outlines, anything less than a superb temperament, can really be said to be quality.

In your judging career, you will meet only a very few dogs of supreme quality although, hopefully, you will handle many quality dogs which will give you moments of great satisfaction.

Necks and throats

1. The neck is muscular and well developed, with a clean throat: Wire Fox Terrier.

2. 'Throaty'. Loose skin under the neck. Incorrect for breeds such as Setters, shown here.

Shoulders and fronts

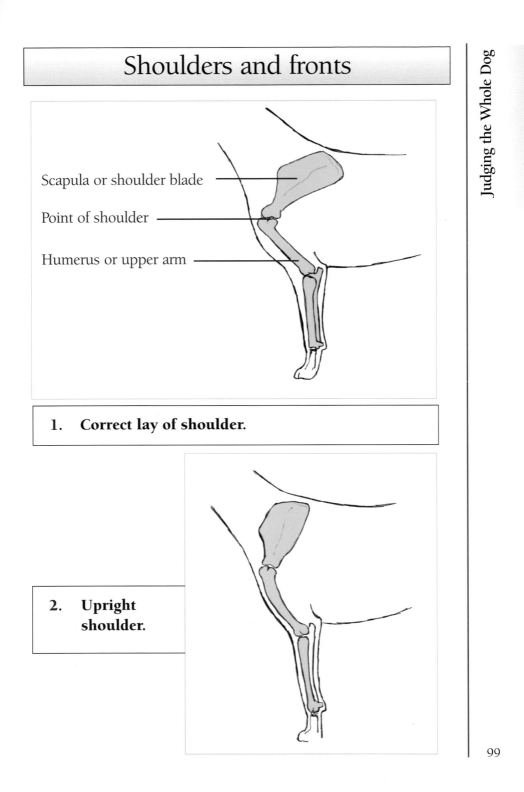

Scapula or shoulder blade

Point of shoulder

Humerus or upper arm

1. Correct lay of shoulder.

2. Upright shoulder.

Shoulders and fronts

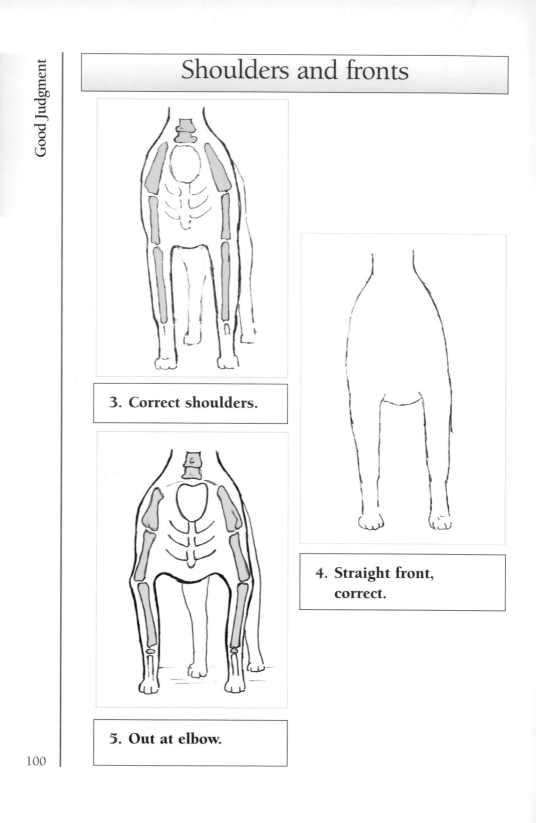

3. Correct shoulders.

4. Straight front, correct.

5. Out at elbow.

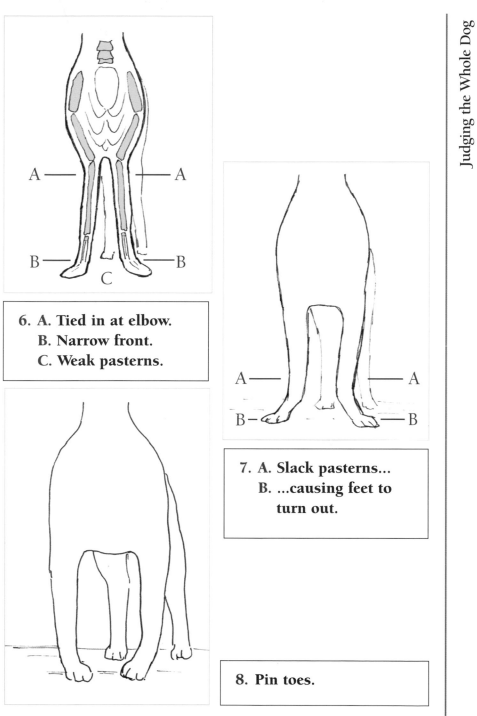

6. A. Tied in at elbow.
   B. Narrow front.
   C. Weak pasterns.

7. A. Slack pasterns...
   B. ...causing feet to turn out.

8. Pin toes.

Chapter Nine

Dressing for the Job

The light that shines upon the judge in a ring has something in it of the power of radium, and it lays bare the soul.

William McCandlish

In The Kennel Club's booklet *Guide for Judges* (a copy of which you should obtain and read carefully), is the following directive: *It is important that judges maintain a proper appearance. They should not be the centre of attention through garish or outlandish dress or through bizarre behaviour.*

It is as well that you remember that, when you are judging, you are as much on show as the dogs. Standing alone in the centre of the ring can make you very vulnerable to the wit of the ringside, so do take a little care over the garments you select.

On the day you are representing your breed, you owe it to the exhibitors and to the officers and committee of the show who invited you to be suitably attired. Jeans and trainers are all right for exercising the dogs and doing the gardening, but they should not be worn for judging by either sex. Hot weather brings out the worst in people when it comes to clothes. Boob tubes or sun tops, especially if worn with short shorts or micro skirts, are not suitable clothing for the lady judge, while men should refrain from taking to the ring in the shorts, T-shirt and espadrilles which they found so comfortable on the beach in Spain! In fact, those judges who bare their bodies under a hot sun are not only offending some of the exhibitors and onlookers but are doing themselves no good, as they will feel far hotter than if they had a light covering and probably will suffer from sunburn.

Winter shows are held indoors, but beware! You go muffled up against the cold only to find that the venue is stiflingly hot. Better to wear a shirt under a sweater which can be discarded if you feel uncomfortable.

It does not look businesslike to judge with your hands in your pockets.

Judges of both sexes must be able to forget their appearance and concentrate solely on the job in hand.

Here are a few tips of dressing for judging.

Men

A well-cut suit is always the most comfortable and suitable garment in which to judge but trousers and a smart blazer, plain or coloured, look neat and workmanlike. Choose a well-fitting shirt and a good tie. Comfort is essential. New shoes are a recipe for disaster, for once your feet start to hurt your concentration goes out of the window!

Avoid strong drink or garlic that lingers on the breath, or hands that smell of tobacco, or a very strong-smelling aftershave. Odours do affect some dogs as their olfactory nerve is much more sensitive than ours.

Do check your flies! I once saw a man judge his whole entry with his flies undone. No one liked to tell him but the whole ringside was rivetted. I do not think they saw the dogs at all and the poor man got dreadfully teased afterwards!

A smartly turned-out judge (Mr Chris Bexon).

Women

Unless you are an exhibitionist and do not care what you show, the length of your skirt is most important. Flared or accordion-pleated skirts can blow up round your waist on a breezy day and, as well as the embarrassment and merriment caused on such occasions, it is plainly impossible to concentrate on the dogs if you have to spend the whole time holding your skirt down. A very tight skirt means you dare not bend to look at the dogs, a short loose skirt rides up as you bend over and an over-long skirt should be avoided because you can trip over the hem.

A skirt or dress with some knife pleats is easiest to wear, and it is quite in order for women to wear a well-fitting trouser suit.

Blouses and dress tops should fit well. Do not have a plunging neckline, it can cause a disturbance!

Keep your coat or jacket buttoned as flapping coats can get in the way when you examine the dogs. Edge to edge styles should be avoided.

Tights or stockings give a nice finish to an outfit, but can be left off in very hot weather.

Do not wear your nails too long, as you might scratch the dog, or even pierce its eye should it jump when being examined. Avoid stiletto heels as it would be easy to step back and perhaps injure a dog's foot. We live in an age of litigation and you could find yourself being sued by an owner if a dog is damaged by your actions, accidental or not.

Avoid dress rings as these can get caught in the coats of long-haired dogs. I once saw a lady judge get one of these rings tangled in the coat of the dog she was examining. She tried hard to unravel it, then the owner tried, then the steward came, all to no avail. After using a rather unladylike expression the judge pulled off the offending bauble and sent the dog away on its triangle with the ring bumping on its neck!

Dangling necklaces can hit a dog's face or get caught around its neck, clashing charm bracelets can disturb puppies, while long, swinging earrings just look out of place. Remember, all eyes are on you so make-up should be complementary, not garish. A story is told of a judge who applied her make-up rather too liberally. During the judging the rain started and one ringsider said to the woman beside her, 'Do you think the rain will make the judge's make-up smudge?' to which the other replied solemnly, 'No, dear, it runs off plastic!' The ringsiders have always been famous for their merry quips. 'Neat and not gaudy' should be the motto.

Women as well as men must think of their feet. Spend time in the shoe shop and buy a pair of well-fitting shoes with a moderate heel, wear them about at home to break them in and then keep them for judging engagements. Unless you live your life in them, high heels can be very tiring when worn for judging.

Rubber or composite soles are recommended for all shoes, because leather soles clatter as you walk up and down the ring at indoor shows and can disturb the dogs.

The author demonstrates appropriate clothing for a windy day.

If you like to wear a hat outside, keep it small and neat. See that it fits well and cannot blow off. Plenty of attractive felts and panamas are on sale at shows. A panama really is a necessity in hot sun, as no one wants to keel over half way through judging due to sunstroke. Hats with a lot of trimming, over-large brims or shallow crowns are a nuisance to manage, and baseball caps worn either way are out!

Quarters

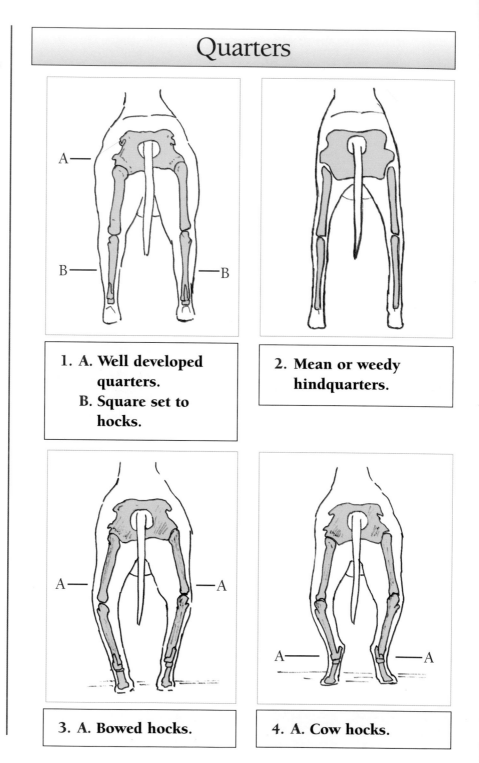

1. **A. Well developed quarters.**
   B. Square set to hocks.

2. **Mean or weedy hindquarters.**

3. **A. Bowed hocks.**

4. **A. Cow hocks.**

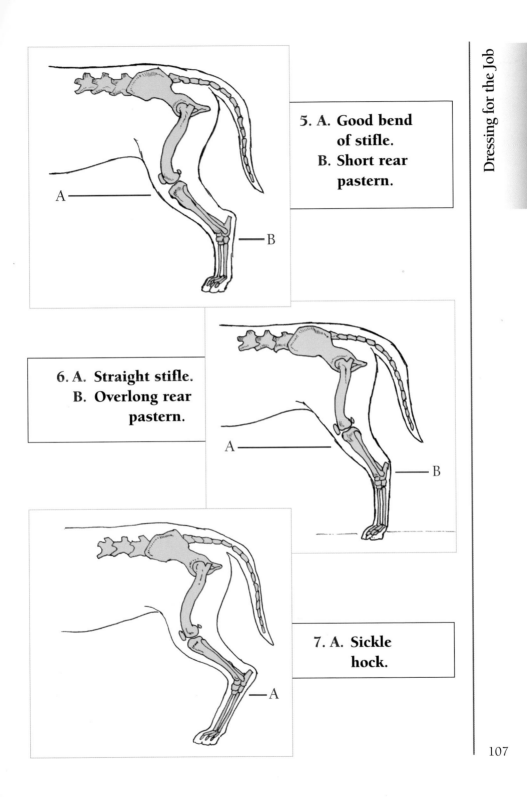

5. A. Good bend
of stifle.
B. Short rear
pastern.

6. A. Straight stifle.
B. Overlong rear
pastern.

7. A. Sickle
hock.

Avoid items such as floating scarves as these will hinder you. Do not use strong perfume. Do not wear dark or tinted spectacles while you are judging, unless there is a medical reason for their use. Your whole outfit should fit well and comfortably and look smart.

Bizarre behaviour

No doubt the persons at The Kennel Club who asked that bizarre behaviour should be avoided were thinking back to one or two of the characters who judged in former days, and who were inclined to go over the top when faced with a packed and amused ringside. There are still one or two about who play to the gallery but the whole process is now much more sober and, at times, quite boring.

You have to remember that many people exhibit their dogs for pleasure, and a cheerful judge who jollies things along can make all the difference to the day. Once I showed at a breed open show where the lady judge never spoke a word the whole day, not even asking the dogs' ages, and speaking neither to dog nor exhibitor. By the time she was half way through, the temperature seemed to have dropped to zero, and we were all in quite a dismal state. It was one of the most depressing shows I ever attended.

You should not engage in a spirited conversation with the exhibitor – there is now a Kennel Club rule which forbids this – but do smile and look as if you are enjoying yourself and are interested in the dogs. You can ask the age of the dog. A word to each dog before you lay hands on it is wise: after all, you are a total stranger to it, so a short introduction breaks the ice.

Never call any exhibitor by their Christian name, no matter how well you know them. They are 'Sir' and 'Madam' in the ring and, when you call them out, do refer to them in this way. Similarly, no exhibitor should call you by your Christian name. These rules of etiquette should be observed in order to have a peaceful ring. Ringsiders and other exhibitors take umbrage if the judge and exhibitor start calling each other 'Jill' or 'Joe' while judging is in progress.

It is unclear what really bizarre behaviour could be. Perhaps The Kennel Club is discouraging streakers, although I know of few judges who would do their image much good by behaving in such a manner! Seriously, avoid loud and uncontrolled laughter, swearing for whatever reason, rudeness to stewards or exhibitors, stopping in the middle of judging to talk to a passing friend, chewing gum, making loud remarks when judging, pulling faces, overdoing gesticulations with hands

Need I say anything more...!

or body, or 'footballers' behaviour' (hugging the winning owner) when the main awards are declared. All these could all come under the heading of bizarre behaviour.

It would also be bizarre to enter the ring in a state of intoxication, although this has been known in the past.

No one but the stewards should be seated at the judge's table, so remember that any friend you take with you must remain at the ringside. It has not been unknown for a friend to be seated at the judge's table actually reading a catalogue, but the practice is strongly discouraged and could, I suppose, come under the heading of 'bizarre'.

Do remember that you too are on show, so dress and behave accordingly.

Head studies

1. **Flatcoated Retriever. All the retriever breeds are required to have sufficient length of foreface to enable them to pick up a bird and carry it carefully and cleanly to the handler.**

2. **The Bulldog. One of the most important parts of this breed is the head. Part of the long description given in the standard reads, 'Jaws broad, massive and square, lower jaw projecting considerably in front of upper and turning up'.**

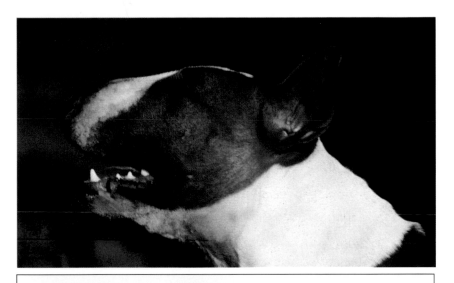

3. The Bull Terrier. The down face of this breed
   makes it instantly recognisable. Part of the breed
   standard on the head reads, 'Profile curves gently
   downwards from top of skull to nose which
   should be black and bent downwards at the tip.'

4. The Whippet. The long, lean skull flat on top
   tapers to the muzzle with a slight stop. The jaws
   are powerful and clean cut.

Judging sight hounds

Sight hounds are essentially galloping breeds. Their deep briskets house powerful hearts and lungs, their strong, wide quarters provide a powerful thrust that engages the correctly laid shoulders and sends the dogs at great speed over the ground. The lithe, muscled body is capable of astonishing twists and turns. These breeds should be viewed and judged as being built to perform such tasks. Sight hounds include Whippets, Greyhounds, Saluki, Afghan, Deerhounds, Irish Wolfhounds, and so on.

1. This Whippet stands over a lot of ground, displays good heart room, strong quarters and good muscling.

2. The Irish Wolfhound should move with a powerful, ground-covering movement which is common to all sight hounds.

Chapter Ten

Dealing with the Hazards

Dog showing is a fine training for the philosophic acceptance of the inevitable, whatever the wish or opinion of the owner, the fiat of the judge goes forth and for that time being is irreversible.

William McCandlish

Call them hazards if you will, but those who take up judging dogs find that many degrees of difficulty are encountered in the job, and the first is the exhibitors themselves!

When you take to the ring to judge your breed for the first time you will find yourself faced by all the people against whom you have shown in the recent past. Some will be your friends, some your enemies. You may know most of the dogs in the ring. However hard (and believe me, until you are faced with this situation you do not realise how hard it is), you must put everything out of your mind but judging the dogs as you see them on the day. Do not let your eyes stray up the lead but keep them firmly fixed on the dogs. Try to put out of your mind all you know or have heard of the exhibits in the months before the show. You can do this if you concentrate hard enough.

Then we come to exhibitors in general. There has been an enormous influx of people into showing and many of them are novices. Some have never owned a dog before, let alone a show dog. Some are there simply because a friend has said of their canine companion, 'Why don't you show him?' So they do. Much of the handling is poor, the dogs are untrained and many of a standard unlikely to make much impact on the prize lists. However, all these dogs are greatly cherished by their owners, who sometimes are unable to understand why their pet has not been placed higher or, perhaps, not placed at all. This is especially true if it has recently won any sort of card.

It is up to the judge to remain calm, pleasant and tactful when

Mr Geoff Corish judging at an outdoor show. All such shows have alternative accommodation in case the weather turns nasty.

confronted by an exhibitor who is irate, tearful or indignant. Questions such as 'Why did you leave my dog out?', or 'Why did I not get placed higher?' should be met with the standard reply, 'On the day I preferred the other exhibits.'

To try to explain why you preferred the other dogs in the class to the questioner's dog can result in unpleasantness. The person who asks for your opinion is rarely seeking the truth, but rather wants to be told how good his dog is. You, as the judge, may feel it necessary, or even helpful, to point out the reasons for your placings, but you must not expect to be thanked.

Another hazard or degree of difficulty lies in the fact that to some extent sentimentality has clogged up the works of dog showing. In the past, if a puppy purchased as a potential show dog did not come up to expectations when fully grown, it would have been given or sold to a suitable pet home and a better type acquired.

With modern pressures, people who buy a puppy hoping it will grow up to be a good winner and then find that it does not come up to expectations feel duty bound to keep it. In many cases these are the dogs that are shown. This fills the rings with many sub-standard specimens, especially in the more popular breeds, and makes the judge's task of sorting the sheep from the goats quite a problem. You will discover, once you have gone over a class, that you have more goats than sheep. However, all exhibitors have paid the same money to enter, and all dogs, good, bad and indifferent, deserve a thorough examination and your entire attention during their moment in the spotlight.

Ringsides also can present a degree of difficulty, as today these are packed with self-acclaimed 'experts' all ready to give an opinion on your performance. These people are not looking at the dogs or appreciating your placings, but are there only in a carping spirit to find some excuse why you did this or that wrong, never acknowledging that the dog at the head of the line was the best on the day.

As a judge, you have to shrug off this bad behaviour, for you will find yourself accused of all manner of crimes, from knowing the exhibitor who stands first (although it is a mystery how, in your own breed, you are expected not to know people with whom you have constant contact on the benches), to using their stud, buying their puppies, entertaining them to lunch and so on. A new judge needs to grow a protective covering very quickly. Try not to be unnerved by the behaviour of ringside critics or, indeed, the behaviour of some exhibitors. Just keep your concentration and refuse to be pushed into doing something that you might regret later. The knowledgeable at your ringside may or may not agree with your decisions, but they are not loud or aggressive and may come up to you afterwards with useful comments that you are wise to accept in the spirit in which they are offered.

If there is a particularly noisy group at your ringside, ask your steward to ask them to move away or tone down their behaviour. Should they refuse, the steward should fetch the show manager to sort this out. Do not take any part yourself, just stop judging and sit down at your table until the matter is settled. Never get into arguments with either ringsiders or exhibitors. If you think a situation is getting out of control, retire to your table and let the show officials sort it out.

Not only can humans get out of control but so can some of the exhibits. In this age of free expression and rights without responsibilities, the idea of making an animal behave in a reasonable manner is anathema to many. Correction in any form is thought to be 'cruel' and an infringement of the animal's liberty. Dogs, like people, are supposed to 'develop naturally' without a kindly hand to guide them to know wrong from right. The consequence is that in many cases the new dog exhibitor, who possibly had no contact with animals before acquiring his puppy, has been afraid to administer any correction as the animal grows up, so the judge is frequently asked to assess a creature which is to all intents and purposes wild and untrained.

If people want to show their dogs, it is up to them to train their animals before entering for a show. You cannot, and should not have to, struggle with an undisciplined dog in the centre of the ring; you are there to judge, not to engage in a wrestling match. The wisest plan is to stop at once from trying to examine an unruly dog: just ask

The shape of feet

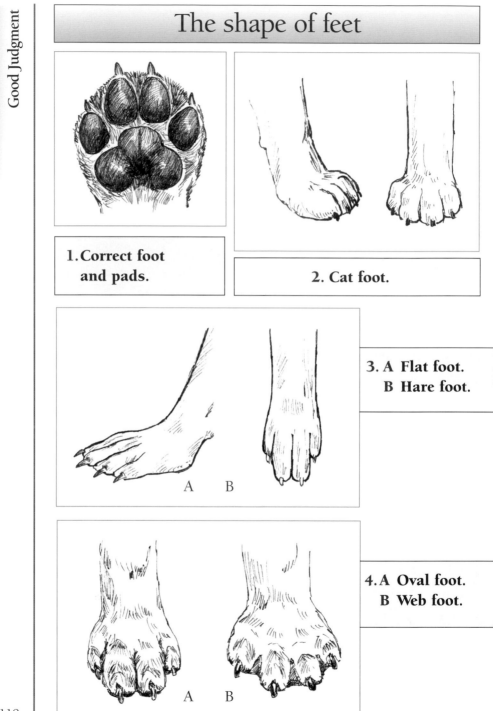

1. **Correct foot and pads.**

2. **Cat foot.**

3. A **Flat foot.**
   B **Hare foot.**

4. A **Oval foot.**
   B **Web foot.**

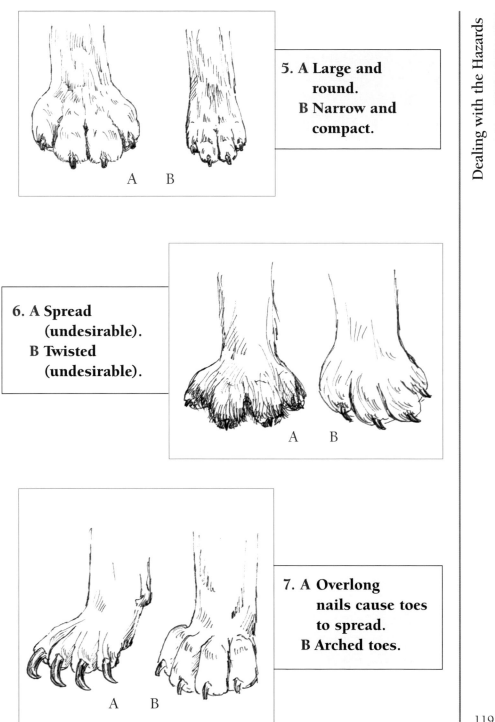

5. A Large and
   round.
   B Narrow and
   compact.

6. A Spread
   (undesirable).
   B Twisted
   (undesirable).

7. A Overlong
   nails cause toes
   to spread.
   B Arched toes.

the exhibitor to move it and then place it back in the line. If you cannot examine a dog properly then it cannot be judged properly and cannot figure in the placings.

Baiting

The way to a dog's heart is through its stomach, which brings me to the next hazard faced by the new judge: feeding in the ring or, to use the American term, 'baiting'.

Many of the long-legged breeds are now subject to what has euphemistically been termed 'crotch feeding'. The handler wears a small pouch strapped to his waist and hanging at crotch level, from which he shovels liver, sausage, cheese, mince and so on unendingly into the dog's mouth in an effort to get it to show off.

Some people bring food in other containers and in one of the breeds I judge it seems that the dogs have their heads permanently in paper bags.

No doubt the exhibitor thinks, mistakenly as it happens, that to feed a dog continuously keeps it on its toes and presents a good outline. Nothing could be further from the truth, as most dogs lean on their forehand and over-stretch the rear. Should the handler be holding a handful of food above the dog's head, its neck is at an angle, with the shoulders open, elbows turned out and the back hollow. If the dog has a tendency to cow hocks, this stance simply accentuates the fault.

In breeds such as the Boxer, where a proud, alert stance is required, it is not unusual for the judge to have lumps of liver or sausage whizzing past his head as the handler strives to get the desired effect!

Even some table dogs now have their mouths crammed with food. It is quite impossible to examine a mouth properly if the dog is eating, and sometimes when you ask the handler to stop feeding it, the dog is so wild to get at the titbits that you are no better off. If you cannot examine the mouth or head properly then you must take this into consideration when making your placings.

Some handlers still wave food about as they go to move their dogs. The consequence of this is that the dog bends its head towards the hand holding the food, the offside shoulder goes out, and it is impossible to assess the dog's movement Again, this is something to remember when choosing your line-up.

Feeding in the ring is an unfair practice as feeders always leave a trail of bits and this does not help the exhibitors who have taken the trouble to train their dogs to show correctly without bribes. Even the best-trained dog is going to lunge at half a juicy sausage.

Difficult show dogs have caused owners agonising moments over how to get a performance out of their reluctant charges. Some owners have resorted to strange methods, entering the ring with something about their person that the dog could not resist and would show for this and for no other reason. Over the years I have met many strange examples, such as the exhibitor who could not get her Setter bitch to show unless she had a kipper stuffed down her bra, or the Spaniel exhibitor who brought a live mouse in a box!

Temperament

The next area of difficulty is temperament. In these days of the Dangerous Dogs Act and constant media attention on dog behaviour, it is imperative that no dog is ever placed whose temperament is less than perfect.

Some dogs rumble in their throats when you handle them. The owner invariably says, 'He's only talking.' My reply is, 'He may be talking to you but he is growling at me!' It has to be said that some dogs do talk under their breath, but look at the expression in their eyes and what their ears are saying and you can tell whether or not the conversation is meant to be pleasant.

If a dog shows any sign of aggression, such as raised hackles, growling, snarling or trying to fight another exhibit, ask that it is taken from the ring. If you do not feel you can do this, put it alone on one side, and at the end of judging put it last in line. If it is a very small class, withhold the card it might have won.

There is a Kennel Club rule designed to deal with savage dogs. If you are bitten when you are judging, send the dog out of the ring immediately. The steward should write down the exhibitor's number and, at the conclusion of judging, the whole matter must be recorded by the secretary who reports it to The Kennel Club. You too should write a report of the incident and post it to The Kennel Club. Failure to make this report can result in you being fined by The Kennel Club.

The reaction of handlers of dogs that shy away, growl or refuse to be handled is always the same: 'He has never done that before!' This is such a standard remark that has become a standing joke among those who judge regularly.

The handler also has numerous other excuses for bad behaviour: 'He has been to the vet.' 'He was bitten when he was coming to the ring.' 'He has been stung by a bee/wasp.' 'We have been on holiday and only just fetched him from the kennels,' and many more.

Many exhibitors try to make the judge responsible for the dog's anti-social stance. I wear a hat when judging outdoors, so it comes in as a very useful object to blame when a dog will not be handled. I have often removed the offending head gear and the dog has not behaved any differently. Now with hotter summers the majority of people have taken to wearing hats, so that excuse is a bit threadbare.

Double handling

We now come to the matter of double handling. Double handling means that the exhibitor places a colleague outside the ring to attract the dog's attention so that it shows better and has an advantage over the exhibits being handled in the accepted manner. It is a Kennel Club rule that no double handling should be allowed, but that does not prevent it from happening. The newer judge must watch out for this and put a stop to it. Be warned, however, that much unpleasantness has been shown to judges trying to stamp out the practice.

Double handling can take many forms, from the unobtrusive call to keys being jangled, the dog's name being shouted, finger snapping, bells ringing, whistle blowing and someone running at speed round the outside of the ring. For some reason it is mostly to be found at the German Shepherd rings, but occasionally it can crop up at ringsides where breeds need to be alert to look their best.

Nip any suggestion of double handling in the bud, firstly by requesting your steward to admonish the participants, and secondly by refusing to continue judging until it has ceased. If you have any trouble, send for the show manager.

These are some of the more usual hazards you will encounter as a judge, but there is no doubt that others will occur as your career unfolds.

Bichon Frisé Ch. Fougere Winging Willie, owned by Mrs N Stapley.

Chapter Eleven

Writing Critiques and Keeping Records

The judge will not be a mirror reflecting the fashion and common talk of the day, but become a force, and a potent force, in the preservation of the breed as a breed.

William McCandlish

Critiques

Although in Britain there is no rule that requires the judge to write a report on the dogs judged, there is a tacit understanding that he will do so. Copies of the reports are sent to the two dog papers, *Dog World* and *Our Dogs*, and appear in print some time during the following six weeks.

In the past, the judge gave a report on the first four dogs placed at every show. However, with the proliferation of shows, breeds and classes, there is simply not enough space to do this today.

The general rule adopted by both dog papers is that for sanction and limited shows only Best in Show, Reserve Best in Show and Best Puppy get a comment. At open shows, the winner of each class gets a report; first and second places are reported at club open shows, general championship, group and breed club championship shows; while for Crufts the first three placings receive a write up.

Not all judges are good at writing reports and sending them in, and letters are always appearing in the dog press from exhibitors who complain about the lack of judges' critiques. However, when the critiques do appear and are candid about what has been shown this, too, causes complaint! Both dog papers give stamped, addressed envelopes to shows for distribution to the judges. These are handed to you with your judge's book, so you have no excuse on that score not to comply with the request for your findings.

Most exhibitors like to know why their dog has been placed

where it was in a class, while others are keen to know for what reason their dog was demoted. When writing your critique, remember this is not only for the owner of the dog but for all those people interested in that particular breed who were not at the show on the day. They like to know what the dogs looked like, so try and be a little descriptive when composing your report.

Do not write your critique with the breed standard beside you, as you may describe the dog as

Ch. Rubicon Reserve, a Border Terrier owned by Mrs Ruth Jordan

having characteristics it does not possess. If you do not know the requirements of your breed well enough to be able to write the report without a crib, then perhaps you are not quite ready to judge.

Keep your first reports short and to the point and do not try to be too clever. Head the report with the name of the show, the location and the date, and sign it. Just say what you have seen and why you liked the winner. Should you have had a poor class, it is in order to say 'this class was a little disappointing', but if you do say this, do not go on to laud the winner of it to the skies, as this is a contradiction in terms. If a dog has a poor mouth but is placed because all the other characteristics please you, say 'has an "if" I do not like', or 'would like a better bite'. Never say outright that the dog's mouth is wrong.

It is always better to qualify any criticism or high praise with the words 'in my opinion', for that is what it is, and if you use this phrase there can be no comeback.

Pick out the best about the dog of which you are writing such as 'best of legs and feet', 'good chiselling round eyes', and do not be afraid to say such things as 'would like a better lay of shoulder', or 'ears could be better set', or 'markings could be clearer', that is, if you truly think so. This is especially necessary if the dog with a fault or failing wins one class and then goes down to second or third in another class. If you have said only how good it is, the owner will wonder why you demoted it in favour of a dog with much the same write up.

Do not fall into the category of those who report every dog as 'nice coat, good body, moved well', being frightened to commit their findings to print. If you are prepared to go in a ring and judge dogs, then you must be prepared to justify your placings.

Do not rush home and write the report straight away. Sleep on it. For the first two or three engagements, you will be on a bit of a high, and reports are better written when you are calmer. Leave the writing for 24 hours until the mist clears and you can actually picture your placed dogs in your mind's eye: then you can give a better idea of them to the readers.

Lay the report on one side for another 24 hours and then go through it again, making any adjustments you think necessary. If possible, reports should be posted to the dog papers within a week of the show date. Keep a copy for yourself as you may need to correct a mistake when it appears in print.

Editors find that typed reports are far easier to deal with, as written ones can be misinterpreted. Many people now have a typewriter, word processor or computer, or know someone who owns one, and it is worth the effort to commit the report to clear typescript.

Records

The keeping of records is very important if you hope one day to have the honour of awarding challenge certificates in your breed (see Chapter 12). These days a very detailed Kennel Club questionnaire is sent out to all judges put up to award tickets for the first time, and the questions in this must be answered correctly. If you have a computer I suggest you make a programme that can be amended each time you judge. If you have a word processor, have a separate disk listing your completed appointments. For those who prefer the written word, buy a large, hard-backed exercise book and rule eight columns, one each for the name of the show, the date, the type of show (sanction, limited or open), breed, number of classes, number of dogs, number of entries, number of absentees.

Fill in the relevant columns after you return from each show. Failure to do this may mean that, when you receive your first questionnaire, you may have wrong or no information for the questions asked. The Judges Sub-Committee at The Kennel Club has only your answers by which to assess your experience, so the more complete your records are, the better.

Never ask anyone else to keep your records, as you and you alone are responsible for their accuracy. You could get into very serious trouble if you made a mistake, however unintentional, when filling in the questionnaire. Set down carefully the numbers of dogs judged and numbers of entries, and be sure you get the correct numbers in the relevant columns. Check and check again.

The questionnaire may also ask what seminars on the breed you have attended, so keep a list of these, with the dates, times and places, and the subjects covered. The keeping of good records is essential in this day and age.

For your own information and interest, keep a cuttings file. Cut out every show report which you write and is published, paste it in a book and date it. It is part of your career as a judge, and in the years to come you will be glad you kept what, in time, becomes a historical reference.

Another scrap book that can be of help and interest is one containing any and every reference to your particular breed found in the press, past and present. You can build up a wonderful record of your breed, its requirements, its merits, its faults and its progress. Cuttings, photographs, photocopies, drawings – anything and everything can be included. These scrap books make a fascinating study of any breed and are invaluable as reference material.

Tails: set, shape and carriage

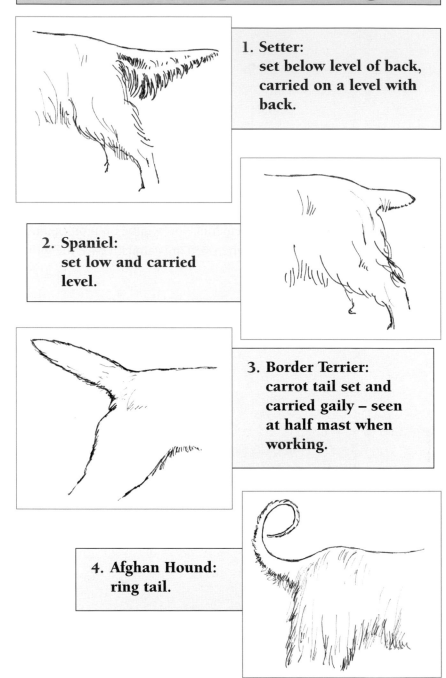

1. **Setter:**
   set below level of back, carried on a level with back.

2. **Spaniel:**
   set low and carried level.

3. **Border Terrier:**
   carrot tail set and carried gaily – seen at half mast when working.

4. **Afghan Hound:**
   ring tail.

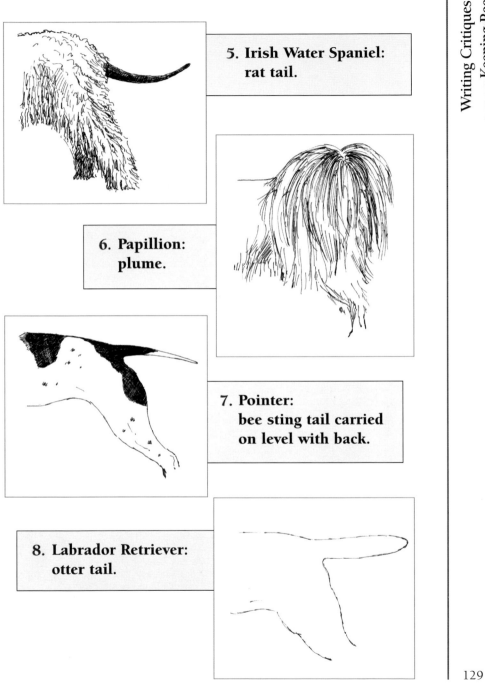

5. **Irish Water Spaniel:**
   rat tail.

6. **Papillion:**
   plume.

7. **Pointer:**
   bee sting tail carried
   on level with back.

8. **Labrador Retriever:**
   otter tail.

Tails: set, shape and carriage

9. **Bernese Mountain Dog:**
   bushy, raised when moving, but never curled or carried over back.

10. **Poodle:**
    tail carried at an angle.

11. **Beagle:**
    tail (stern) set high.

12. **Pug:**
    twist.

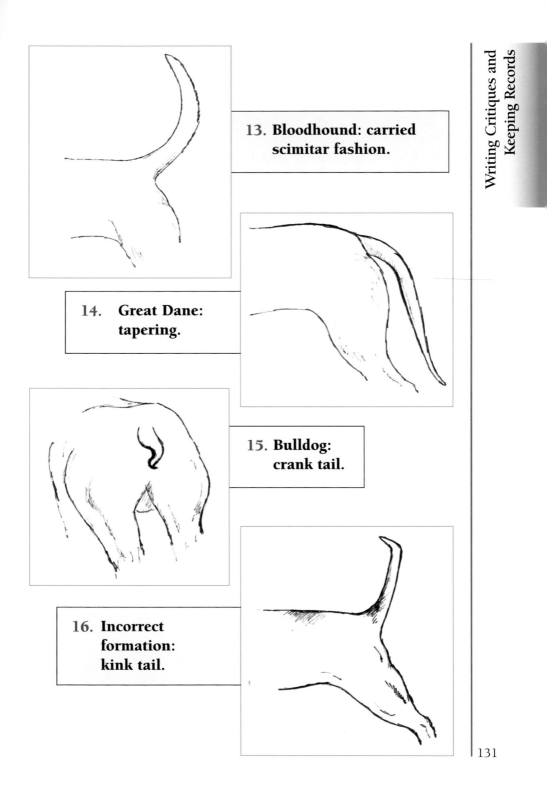

13. **Bloodhound: carried scimitar fashion.**

14. **Great Dane: tapering.**

15. **Bulldog: crank tail.**

16. **Incorrect formation: kink tail.**

Chapter Twelve

The Next Steps

The best of judges will make mistakes, incompetent judges may set shoulders shrugging, inexperienced judges must try their 'prentice hands, unfair judges may occasion whisperings and scandal, but in the end, the dog will have his day.

William McCandlish

After about five or six years of judging, when you are seen to be a good, straightforward judge with knowledge and interest in the job, you will probably be invited to judge at a breed club open show. This is a big step forward for the journeyman judge who hopes, one day, to be passed to award challenge certificates in his chosen breed.

The club open show is a supreme test of stamina and concentration, for you will have to go over more dogs of your own breed than ever before. How you acquit yourself is noted by those who will consider whether you are suitable to award challenge certificates in the future. Your showing may also decide whether you advance from the club B list to the A2, where your name could be put forward when a judge is needed for a championship show. When you have been passed by The Kennel Club, you are then placed on the A1 list.

If you judge your breed in an honest and straightforward manner, taking into consideration the requirements of soundness, type and quality, and arrive at a result without fear or favour, you will be appreciated by those truly interested in the breed. You may lose a few friends and may even make a few enemies, but those who put the breed first and their own ambitions second will applaud your decisions and you will benefit in the long run.

After you have judged your breed at a number of open shows, you will be invited to take on other breeds within your group. Do make a thorough study of them before accepting an invitation. Do not accept any breed unless you are sure that you know enough about its Standard to be able to come up with the right decisions.

One day, you will be invited to judge a championship show, and a dog like German Shepherd Ch. Mirabos Atlantic Breeze may be your choice of champion.

The morning when the postman brings the first invitation to judge your breed at a championship show and award challenge certificates will go down in your calendar as a red letter day! Accept the invitation in the usual way, and the secretary of the show will send you The Kennel Club questionnaire which you must complete with absolute accuracy. If you are in any doubt about any show you have judged, numbers of classes and so on, do not make a guess, but simply put 'no record'. However, if you have kept the records of your show career accurately, as I have advised, you should have all the details at your fingertips.

Take plenty of time to fill in this form and check it several times before posting it back. You might have to wait some months before you hear whether you have been passed by the Judges Sub-Committee for the engagement. Possess your soul in patience, and do not ring up the show secretary or, for that matter, The Kennel Club, in an endeavour to find out the result. Just wait. You will receive a letter from the show secretary advising you when he has been notified by The Kennel Club that you have been passed.

It is a great thrill to see your name in print in the *Kennel Gazette* cited as a breed judge for a championship show. An asterisk beside it indicates that it is your first championship show assignment.

Some time before the show you will receive a copy of the schedule, car pass, complimentary entrance ticket, details of the hotel if you are staying overnight and, possibly, an expense sheet to be completed and handed in at the treasurer's office on the show day.

On the day of the show, arrive at least half an hour before judging begins. If the show is held in conjunction with a well-known agricultural show such as Three Counties or East of England, it is wise to get there at about 8.00 am, as otherwise you might get held up in traffic jams for at least two hours. It is far better to arrive early than be fuming in traffic and arriving hot and bothered or, worse, late. If you live over 100 miles from the venue, do accept the Society's offer of a hotel room the night before. However close to the show ground you are staying, remember the traffic, so rise early, have a decent breakfast and get there before the rush hour.

On arriving at the show, go straight to the secretary's office and check in. Either from there or from reception you collect your envelope or pouch with your name, the breed you are judging and your ring number on the cover. It contains the judge's book and badge, hand wipes, press envelopes, challenge certificates, reserve challenge certificates, BOB card, rosettes for the top winners, cards from pet food firms who have donated prizes, lunch ticket and, possibly, a pen.

You are then directed to the judges' reception area where tea, coffee and biscuits are dispensed, and you will be welcomed by a member of the committee. These areas are jokingly referred to by the cognoscenti as 'hostilities'! Certainly there can be the odd incident, but mostly they are friendly, jolly places where you meet many people you know already and make new acquaintances. The dog press generously supply free copies of their papers, so you have a chance to relax while you look at these at your leisure, or talk to a fellow judge.

Go through your folder, and acquaint yourself with the contents. Do not sign the challenge certificates. This is quite out of order. If they are mislaid or stolen before the awards have been made there is no knowing to what use they will be put by those unscrupulous enough to have stolen them in the first place.

Ten minutes before judging, make your way to your ring, where you will find your stewards waiting at the judging table. There are usually two stewards to each ring at a championship show, one to keep the ring going (known as the 'judge's steward'), and one at the table to keep the paperwork up to date.

Your judging book is larger than the one used at open shows, and has four columns, one for you, one for the secretary's office, one for the ring award board and one for the general award board. Do check at the conclusion of each class that you have correctly filled in all the columns, signed them, torn them out and handed them to the steward. This is especially true of the last sheet of slips, usually coloured, which is reserved for the numbers of challenge certificates, reserves and Best of Breed winners. In the general excitement this

Toplines

1. Level topline: Beagle.

2. Characteristic topline of breeds such as the Italian Spinone and the Chesapeake Bay Retriever. Dip behind the shoulders (A).

A

3. Balanced outline: Cocker Spaniel. Good neck and shoulders and well-developed quarters. Good level topline.

4. **Unbalanced: the dog has all weight on the forehand (A) and is weak in the quarters (B).**

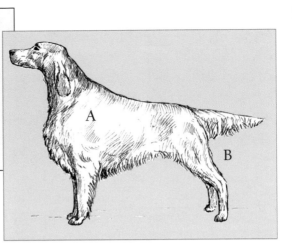

5. **Setter: Overlong in the loin (A) leading to dip in topline (B).**

6. **The legs on this Poodle are too far forward, indicating upright shoulders. Heavy-coated breeds must be handled by the judge to ascertain conformation.**

page is often forgotten, so the steward has to chase you round the ground after the judging to retrieve the missing sheet. Always check to see that all the slips have been handed in.

Naturally you will feel nervous, as awarding a challenge certificate is a big responsibility, but your pleasure in the event should outweigh your panic. Once you have started to judge, you will forget your nerves and enjoy the task ahead.

If you are judging both sexes, you will be asked if and when you wish to take a lunch break. Personally, if the entry does not exceed 100 dogs, I prefer to judge the whole entry without a break. This enables you to consider the entry without interruptions and keep your concentration. Coffee can be taken at your table between classes. However, a larger number of dogs does mean long hours in the ring, so you may prefer to break between the sexes, and it is up to you to say how long you intend to take for lunch. My own personal feeling is, the shorter the break, the better; firstly, because people and dogs have already been there some time and should not be kept waiting until they are tired and fed up and, secondly, because once you lose concentration it takes a little while for it to come back again. I would say that 30 to 45 minutes is quite long enough, although many judges do like an hour and some shows insist on this. The table steward writes your decision on the blackboard for all to see, such as '30-minute break between sexes', or 'lunch break one to two', or 'back at 1.30', and so on.

Do not discuss your judging with anyone during the lunch break. Eat sparingly as you do not want to be overfull and sluggish for the afternoon's work. One glass of wine is sufficient. The days when it was said of some judges, 'They are great judges before lunch!' are, hopefully, over.

There is no hard and fast rule that says you have to award the dog CC at the conclusion of the dog judging. In some gundog breeds this cannot be done, as often there is a class for Field Trial competitors of both sexes at the end of the bitch judging. The winner of this is eligible to compete for the CC and may be a dog. However, it is far more satisfactory to be able to judge the dog CC at the conclusion of the dog judging and before any bitches have been in the ring, as their scent does distract many males who then do not show well.

All judge's books contain a slip instructing the judge not to award the challenge certificates unless the dog is of such outstanding merit as to be worthy of the title of champion. If the CC is withheld, then the reserve CC must also be withheld, but the judge must still make a Best of Breed. It is very seldom that challenge certificates are withheld, but it is not unknown, especially in breeds of small numbers.

Hopefully, you will not be presented with this dilemma on your big day, and you will be faced by a line-up for the coveted 'ticket' that pleases you and you will be able to choose your top winners with confidence.

All unbeaten class winners are called in to compete for the challenge certificate, and there is a rider that says the judge may also call in any other dog. So if in your own mind you have decided to award the CC to, say, the post-graduate winner and you like the second in the class almost as much, you can ask the steward to bring that dog in, or at least have it standing on the sideline, so that it can be called in when the CC has been awarded to challenge for reserve. However, there is no rule that says you must call in the second prize winner from the class won by the CC winner to challenge for the reserve certificate.

Once the CC and reserve CC have been awarded, cards and rosettes are handed out and the winners do a lap of honour before coming back to your table where you fill in and sign the certificates. Please do not leave the name of the dog and owner blank, as again the cards may be lost or stolen and put to uses other than that intended.

Both dog and bitch CC winners come in to compete for Best of Breed and should be moved with the dog leading the bitch. The BOB card must also be filled in and signed and you must write down the sex of the winner.

If your breed is one of the more popular and a judge is engaged for each sex, you have to come together to decide BOB. This may be slightly intimidating if your co-judge is very famous in the breed. Do remember, though, that you are considered experienced enough to judge at the same level, so think hard when examining both dogs and do not give way lightly if you really prefer your own choice. However, you must be able to explain clearly why you have come to that decision. In the event of the two judges not coming to an agreement, the referee is sent for.

While the referee is busy, stand by your table and do not make any comments. The referee will hand the BOB card to his choice but both you and your co-judge sign the card.

Best puppy is then judged either by you alone or with your co-judge if there is one. If you disagree then the referee steps in again.

After the judging, please remember to thank your stewards before making your way to lunch or to reception for a cup of tea before setting off home. Remember to hand in your expense sheet and to thank the secretary.

Finally, do drive home carefully. You will be physically exhausted but on quite a high, with the dogs and your placings rushing through your brain. I strongly recommend a short break in reception or, if you can spare the time, at the top table in the ring to watch the group and support your BOB.

Judging overseas

From this engagement might spring an invitation to judge overseas. This is an entirely new situation, as most of the countries are affiliated to the FCI (Fédération Cynologique Internationale), where things are very different from the scene in Britain. There are different methods of judging, all kinds of awards we do not have and, as well as CCs, you have to award the CACIB, the international certification. All dogs have to be graded in this way: excellent, very good, good, poor or unable to be judged. In most continental and Scandinavian countries you have to dictate a description of each dog in the entry to a 'secretary' at your table, and there are endless slips, forms and certificates to sign.

In the United States of America, the classes are timed, and you have a time sheet to fill in. It is also your responsibility to check the ring numbers of the competitors. In Australia, speed is of the essence and, as soon as you line up one class for awards, the next is ready behind you. Rings must run to time, as there is a whole batch of hotly-contested 'property classes' at the end which have to be judged carefully. In neither country are you required to give either verbal or written reports, although if you are judging a 'specialty', that is, a breed show, the club may ask if you would comment for the year book or magazine.

Whatever country you are invited to, get a copy of their judging procedure and awards, and a copy of the breed standard which may differ in some respects from our own.

For all overseas engagements, travelling is tiring, evening meals are late and a good night's sleep is imperative. Unless you are fit and active, carefully consider all the options before accepting overseas invitations. The show day is long, and all judges are expected to watch the group judging which can go on for over two hours. They are also expected to attend the official dinner, which starts at a fairly late hour and includes speeches. It is a great social occasion, however, and can go on well into the night.

Many overseas venues are huge so there is quite a lot of walking. Lunch is taken after the judging, which may be as late as 4.00 pm if the entry is up to the limit. No judge is allowed more than a certain number of dogs in any one day as, with all the writing to be done, there is just not the time to allow anyone to take on the number they would judge in Britain.

In conclusion

I hope that you have enjoyed reading this book and that it will help you to achieve your ambition of becoming a judge. At times you may be discouraged, or feel that you cannot do the job properly. Persevere, and you will find that it all falls into place.

To all who don the judge's mantle, good luck, and I hope that you have as much pleasure and satisfaction as I have derived from my life with dogs.

Index

A page number in **bold type** indicates that the entry takes the form of photographs or drawings to illustrate its meaning.